Early Civilizations

Early Civilizations
Ancient Egypt in Context

Bruce G. Trigger

The American University in Cairo Press

First paperback printing 1995

Dar el Kutub No. 3191/95
ISBN 977 424 365 X

Printed in Egypt at the Printshop of the American University in Cairo

Contents

Preface

This book is based on four lectures on "Ancient Egypt as an Early Civilization" that I delivered at the American University in Cairo between April 12 and 15, 1992, while I was Distinguished Visiting Professor in the Department of Sociology, Anthropology, and Psychology. My thanks go to the American University in Cairo for this opportunity to return to Egypt and particularly to Professor Kent Weeks and his wife Susan for their unstinting hospitality to my wife and myself throughout our three-week stay. I also wish to thank George Gibson, the Provost of AUC, and other members of the university and the Cairo archaeological community for helping to make our visit a memorable one.

The task I was assigned was to encourage Egyptologists to develop a comparative interest in other early civilizations and at the same time to help bring the study of ancient Egypt back into the mainstream of comparative anthropology. I attempted to do this by considering some of the ways in which ancient Egypt resembled other early civilizations as well as some of the ways in which it was unique. The positive response to my lectures makes me hope that there will be a receptive audience for this book. In preparing my lectures for publication, I have tried to preserve as much as possible of their original style and organization.

My long-standing interest in the comparative study of early civilizations has been reflected in an undergraduate course titled "The Social Institutions of Early Civilizations" that I have taught at McGill University since the 1960s. For the last three years I have been working full-time on a comparative study of seven early civilizations, hoping to reveal more about the nature of factors which constrain human behavior. During the calendar years 1990 and 1991 I was relieved from most teaching and all administrative duties at McGill University by a Killam Research Fellowship administered by the Canada Council. During 1992 I have continued to benefit from McGill University's enlightened policy of sabbatical leaves.

The present work, besides comparing ancient Egypt with six other early civilizations, constitutes an interim report on my findings to date. Over the next few years I hope to publish two more books based on my current research. One will provide synoptic descriptions of the seven civilizations that I am investigating; the other will offer a detailed analysis of how and why these civilizations resembled and differed from each other.

The theoretical structure of the present book evolved in the course of preparing two earlier lectures on my research. The first was given informally in the Department of Archaeology at the University of Bergen, Norway, while I was visiting that university as a guest of the Center for the Study of the Sciences and the Humanities in February 1991. The second lecture, titled "Constraint and Freedom in the Shaping of Early Civilizations: A Working Paper," was delivered a year later in the Department of Anthropology at the University of Toronto, during a visit sponsored by the Snider Lectureship Fund. I wish to thank in particular Professors Randi Haaland and Nils Gilje at the University of Bergen and Professor Richard B. Lee at the University of Toronto for making these visits possible.

The present work has benefited substantially from comments received in both Bergen and Toronto, but especially from the questions and discussions that followed my lectures in Cairo. I am particularly grateful to Susan Weeks for her penetrating questions, to Dr. Joan Oates for valuable comments, and especially to Dr. Barbara Welch for reading and commenting on a draft of the book. The final version of the chronological chart was drawn by Simon N. O'Rourke, and he and Arnold C. Tovell have played indispensable roles in guiding my manuscript through press.

I would finally like to acknowledge the inspiration I have derived from the work of Robert McC. Adams. His approach, more than that of any other anthropologist, has inspired and influenced my study of early civilizations.

Comparative Chronological Chart of Early Civilizations
(see over)

Date	Mesopotamia	Egypt	North China	Maya Lowlands	Basin of Mexico	Peru — Coast	Peru — Highlands	Southwestern Nigeria
A.D. 1500	Achaemenid	Late Period	Eastern Chou	Late Postclassic	Late Aztec	Chimu	Inka	Yoruba Civilization
A.D. 1000	Neo-Babylonian			Early Postclassic	Early Aztec		(chiefdoms and small states)	
A.D. 500	Middle Babylonian	New Kingdom	Western Chou	Terminal Classic / Late Classic	Toltec		Huari Tia-huanaco	
A.D./B.C.	Kassite		Late Shang	Early Classic	Teotihuacan	Moche		
B.C. 500				Late Preclassic			Chavin de Huantar	
B.C. 1000	Old Babylonian / Isin-Larsa / Ur III / Akkadian	Middle Kingdom	Early Shang					
B.C. 1500			Erh-li-t'ou			Sechin Alto		
B.C. 2000	Early Dynastic III	Old Kingdom						
B.C. 2500	Early Dynastic I/II							
B.C. 3000	Jemdat Nasr	Early Dynastic Period						
B.C. 3500	Late Uruk							

Comparative Chronological Chart of Early Civilizations
(previous page)

Solid lines show beginnings and ends of civilizations; shaded bands show periods discussed in this book. The Maya, Aztec, and Inka civilizations were terminated by Spanish conquest. Yoruba civilization continues to the present, but was transformed into a modern industrial society beginning at the end of the nineteenth century. The dates selected as marking the transition from early to later preindustrial civilization in Mesopotamia, Egypt, and China tend to be arbitrary. For the first two I have selected their conquest by Alexander the Great, which was quickly followed by major economic and political changes. In the case of Egypt, however, economic and political civilization were already underway in the Late Period, while major elements of the Egyptian religion survived until the country's conversion to Christianity. For China, I have selected the middle of the Eastern Chou period (c. 550 B.C.) as marking the end of early civilization as defined in this book. The Peruvian cultural entities labeled Sechin Alto and Chavin de Huantar may have been early states or chiefdoms rather than early civilizations. There is at least a possibility that the postclassic Maya had reached the level of a later preindustrial civilization. (Schele and Freidel 1990).

One

The Unique and the General

> ... concerning Egypt I will now speak at length, because nowhere
> are there so many marvelous things, nor anywhere else on earth
> are there to be seen so many works of inexpressible greatness.
>
> Herodotus, *History* II.35

Already in Herodotus' time Egypt was recognized as an ancient civilization. Its extraordinary accomplishments commanded the wonder and admiration of foreign visitors, while many of its customs astonished and even shocked them. Yet ancient Egypt was only one of many civilizations that developed independently of each other in different parts of the world beginning about five thousand years ago.

This book will consider ancient Egypt in the light of comparative research I am doing on it and six other early civilizations. It will try to delineate what features ancient Egypt had in common with other early civilizations and to what extent it was unique. The first chapter is a theoretical and methodological introduction and the following three chapters deal with the economies, political organization, and religious aspects of early civilizations. A final chapter considers briefly the relevance of these comparisons for understanding the factors which shaped the development of these societies.

The Comparative Study of Early Civilizations

Except in relation to the study of the early development of the Egyptian state, where anthropological archaeologists such as Walter

1

Fairservis (1972), the late Michael Hoffman (1979), Robert Wenke (1989), and anthropologically informed Egyptologists such as Kathryn Bard (1987, 1992) play a major role, relations between Egyptology and anthropology have not been as close as they should be, or even as close as contacts between the two disciplines were in the more remote past. Egyptology began as, and has largely remained, a humanistic study of the past. It is characterized by a deep interest in philology, art history, and to a lesser degree political history. This has not ruled out a concern with everyday life, as was demonstrated long ago by the works of J. Gardner Wilkinson (1854) and Adolf Erman (1894). Yet, except in the archaeological researches of W.M. Flinders Petrie (Drower 1985), the study of everyday life in ancient Egypt has not been a central concern. Its understanding has been treated as something that emerges naturally out of familiarity with the data, rather than as a form of investigation that requires special training, as philology and art history do. Egyptologists tend to assume that no particular expertise is needed to understand the behavior of the ancient Egyptians. Yet they are also convinced that ancient Egyptian civilization was unique and should be studied for its own sake. According to Christopher Eyre (1987a:5), the belief that Egyptian civilization was different from that of any other society has discouraged Egyptologists from treating information about other early civilizations as a means to understand ancient Egypt better.

Anthropologists long shared a similar, strong commitment to historical particularism, although they combined it with a greater acceptance of cultural relativism. Early in the twentieth century the German-born American anthropologist Franz Boas convinced most of his colleagues that every culture was a unique product of its own largely fortuitous historical development and hence could be studied and appreciated only in terms of its own beliefs and values (Harris 1968:250–89).

Yet in the 1960s anthropological archaeology was inspired by cultural–ecological and neoevolutionary tendencies in social anthropology to abandon its traditional commitment to historical particularism and begin paying greater attention to the cross-cultural regularities in human behavior, which soon became privileged objects of study. Beginning in the 1930s, the cultural ecologist Julian Steward maintained that the comparative examination of regularities in human behavior should be the primary object of social science research, while stigmatizing as parochial the investigation of traits that were specific only to historically related cultures (Steward 1949). Steward's ecological approach stressed the importance of studying what was cross-culturally recurrent and ignoring what was unique. The processual archaeology of the 1960s, which embodied Steward's program, stressed the study of ecology, trade, and sociopolitical organization, while treating art, religion, and values as epiphenomenal and hence of little real interest. Contrary to the Boasian position, science and the evolutionary study of the general were privileged at the expense of history and the investigation of the particular (Caldwell 1959; Watson, LeBlanc, and Redman 1971; Binford 1972).

The supporters of this paradigm made important methodological contributions to the study of archaeological data and the understanding of early civilizations. Yet, despite Steward's formal commitment to multilinear evolution, the major works of this period, even when they did not have a processual orientation, tended to treat all early civilizations as developing along similar lines. This was true of Steward's "Cultural Causality and Law: A Trial Formulation of the Development of Early Civilizations" (1949), Robert McC. Adams' *The Evolution of Urban Society: Early Mesopotamia and Prehispanic Mexico* (1966), and Paul Wheatley's *The Pivot of the Four Quarters* (1971), a comparative study of urbanism in preindustrial civilizations.

Only in the 1980s did anthropological archaeologists once again become concerned with the many aspects of human endeavors, and hence of the archaeological record, that were being ignored as a result of this nearly exclusive preoccupation with cross-cultural regularities. There also developed a renewed appreciation for the considerable variation in human behavior from one culture to another. Within the context of what has come to be called postprocessual archaeology, religion, art, values, and people's perceptions of themselves and the world around them came to be viewed as important elements in understanding human behavior and accounting for the archaeological record (Flannery and Marcus 1976; Hodder 1986, 1987a, 1987b; Shanks and Tilley 1987; Bintliff 1991; Preucel 1991). A widespread acceptance of ecological factors as the principal determinants of human behavior was increasingly replaced by a neo-Boasian cultural determinism, which posited that beliefs transmitted in specific cultural traditions are the main factors influencing human behavior. This approach values the study of the beliefs of other peoples more than it does the search for general explanations of human behavior (Wylie 1985:90).

Such developments have been encouraged by a renewed emphasis in social anthropology on seeing cultural traditions as 'sense-making systems' that shape people's perceptions and values—hence fundamentally influencing their reactions to new experiences. Through the advocacy of scholars such as Victor Turner (1967, 1975), Marshall Sahlins (1976), and Clifford Geertz (1984), these ideas have acquired enormous influence among social anthropologists. This development in turn has convinced many archaeologists that the distinctions that processual archaeologists had drawn between science and history, evolution and history, and the social sciences and humanities are unproductive and misleading, and henceforth should be abandoned. Many archaeologists have also become convinced that it is as important to try to explain behavioral differences among peoples as it is to explain similarities. Those postprocessual archaeologists who do not deny the value of all comparative studies have restored to comparative research the goals it had when an earlier generation of scholars, including V. Gordon Childe (1934), Henri Frankfort (1948, 1956), and Karl Wittfogel (1957), exhibited an interest in the differences as well as the similarities among early civilizations.

My own work is premised on the assumption that, when it comes to accounting for human behavior, explaining differences is theoretically as important as explaining similarities. Even aspects of behavior that are unique to individual civilizations should be studied. For example, many peoples have conceptualized "high places" as points where human beings can gain privileged access to the supernatural. Only the ancient Egyptians, however, drawing upon the imagery of islands of high ground emerging from the annual Nile flood, formulated the specific concept of the mound of creation, upon which order emerged from the primeval sea at the time of creation and where it was recreated at the beginning of each day and every time a pharaoh sat upon his throne. This unique concept resonated throughout ancient Egyptian religious thought. The mound of creation underlay the heart of every temple and inspired the pyramids and obelisks that to outsiders have become the symbols of Egyptian civilization. The full meaning of such symbols can be understood only through the detailed contextual study of ancient Egyptian beliefs and practices, not through the comparison of ancient Egypt with other early civilizations.

Yet Egyptian civilization also shared important features with many other early civilizations and in some instances with all of them. Kingship, taxes, and bureaucracy are only a few traits that are found in all early civilizations. The identification and explanation of such common features help scholars to understand every early civilization better. This is especially important since, because of a lack of information, there is much that we do not know about individual early civilizations. A comparative study of the traits common to all, or even some, of the early civilizations may assist us to understand ancient Egypt better. At the same time, the features unique to ancient Egypt are equally important for understanding all other early civilizations.

The concept of early civilization as a distinctive type of society implies an evolutionary view of human history. Social evolutionism has been sharply attacked in recent decades as a myth that was created by Western European scholars beginning in the eighteenth century to justify colonial exploitation in many parts of the world (Sioui 1992). I do not dispute that there is truth in this charge, but would question the further suggestion that evolutionism, as an approach to studying human history, is inherently and inescapably colonialist or racist. In recent decades archaeological research which has been inspired by an evolutionary perspective has demonstrated the creativity and progress achieved in prehistoric times by indigenous peoples around the world. Especially since the 1960s, knowledge of their achievements has played a significant role in undermining the justifications offered for colonialism and has helped to encourage independence movements in many countries (Robertshaw 1990).

It is also unrealistic to deny the fact of cultural evolution. All modern societies are descended from Palaeolithic hunter–gatherer societies. Along the way, those that have abandoned hunter–gatherer economies have also experienced major changes in social organization and in the way their members perceive the universe and the place of human beings in it. Evolutionary beliefs cause harm when anthropologists become so preoccupied with evolutionary change that they forget the common humanity of all peoples and deny cultural relativism to the extent that they fail to remember, for example, that groups that have remained hunter–gatherers have as much right as anyone else to have their ways of life respected and that these peoples may, like all others, possess understanding and knowledge that are potentially valuable for all humanity.

To adapt cultural evolutionism to a modern scientific understanding of human behavior, it is necessary to stop viewing it as a unilinear process, with all societies evolving along a single path to a common future. When it came to the study of early civilizations, Julian Steward was a unilinear evolutionist to the same degree as were most evolutionists of the nineteenth century (Steward 1949). In the period following World War II, this was also true of Leslie White (1949, 1959), neoevolutionary anthropologists such as Elman Service (1971, 1975) and Morton Fried (1967), and most processual archaeologists. In each instance unilinear evolutionism was based on an unrealistic faith in the cross-cultural regularity of human behavior.

My own view of cultural evolution is more pragmatic and inductive. I acknowledge that new forms of societies have come into being during the course of human history and that it is important to understand the distinctive properties of each new type of society and how it has affected existing ones. Like the American anthropologist George P. Murdock (1959) and the British archaeologist V. Gordon Childe (1947), I see cultural evolution as being congruent with the sum total of human history and the task of anthropologists to explain both the similarities and the differences that have characterized that history. An evolutionism that seeks to account only for similarities destines itself to be incomplete.

A Definition of Early Civilization

Early civilization, as anthropologists use this term, denotes the earliest form of class-based society that developed in the course of human history. Early civilizations constitute the first but not the only type of preindustrial civilization (Crone 1989). They are (or rather were, since none currently exists) characterized by a high degree of social and economic inequality; power was based primarily on the creation and control of agricultural surpluses. While the technologies of these societies tended to remain simple, the organization and management of human labor could sometimes be quite complex. These societies were internally stratified in a hierarchy of largely endogamous classes. Each civilization was based upon exploitative relations, in which a king and a small ruling class extracted surplus production from the lower classes. These surpluses supported an elite style of life that was clearly distinguished from that of the lower classes by its luxuriousness and by the creation of monumental art, architecture, and other status symbols. Both slavery and coercive institutions, such as corvée labor and mandatory military service, existed, but they were less developed than in many subsequent preindustrial societies. Yet those in control possessed sufficient political power and social sanctions to conserve the stability of their regimes over long periods. The symbols that were used to conceptualize and discuss social relations in such societies were drawn mainly from the sphere of religion, which at its highest levels was subject to state control (Sahlins 1976:211–12). In these societies distinctions that are drawn today between the natural, the supernatural, and the social had little, if any, meaning.

In the past, civilization has often been equated with literacy (Morgan 1907:12; Childe 1950; Sjoberg 1960:32–34, 38; Goody 1986). Yet this association does not hold any more than do attempts to define early civilizations in terms of other specific traits of material culture. In Egypt, Mesopotamia, China, and among the Mayas of Central America, fully developed writing systems, based on logographic, phonetic, and semantic—but not on purely syllabic or alphabetic—principles, were created at an early stage in the development of civilization. In highland Mexico, despite considerable emphasis on record keeping for economic and historical purposes, no means was developed for representing speech, as opposed to ideas, and in Peru and West Africa no indigenous system of writing was ever developed. Yet there is no obvious difference in the degree of social, economic, and political development of early civilizations according to whether or not they possessed writing. The Inkas developed an elaborate system of *quipus*, or knotted cords, as mnemonics for keeping government accounts, and where it was not possible to record speech professional 'rememberers' kept track of the past and of other vital information for the upper classes. It is interesting that in each civilization where writing appears to have developed without any evident outside stimulus, it did so at an early phase in the history of that civilization. On the other hand, despite a long tradition of idea-writing in highland Mexico, the peoples of that region did not develop true literacy prior to the Spanish conquest.

Anthropologists distinguish early civilizations from less complex chiefdoms or tribal states and from still simpler tribal agricultural and hunter–gatherer societies. These smaller-scale societies tended to be integrated primarily by kinship networks, and social relations rather than religious concepts played a leading role in mediating all other forms of activities (Fried 1967; Service 1971). Early civilizations were also different from later, more complex preindustrial societies, such as those of classical Greece, Rome, and Han China, where wealth was calculated more abstractly in terms of money rather than land, money payments tended to replace corvées and payments in kind, armies became institutionalized to the point where their commanders might challenge the power of the state, and international religions developed in a context in which the natural, supernatural, and social realms became increasingly differentiated (Heichelheim 1958). Early civilizations are also distinguished from still later forms of preindustrial civilization, such as the feudal societies of medieval Europe and Japan. It is doubtful that any of these later forms of preindustrial civilizations could have evolved had early civilizations not previously arisen in the same or adjacent regions.

City and Territorial States

All of the early civilizations that I have studied can be subdivided into two general types according to the nature of their political organization. I have labeled these city-state systems and territorial states (Trigger 1985a). Charles Maisels (1990) has called them city and village states.

City-state systems took the form of a network of adjacent city states whose elites tended to compete with one another, often militarily, to control territory, trade routes, and other resources, while at the same time sharing common status symbols and making alliances with each other, often through intermarriage among their ruling families. Each city state had a relatively small territory (often covering only a few hundred square kilometers) and a capital city, which frequently was enclosed by a wall. In addition to its capital, a city state might have a number of smaller centers as well as numerous farming villages and hamlets. The four city-state systems that I consider in this study are those of ancient Sumer, located in southern Mesopotamia (Iraq), prior to the Old Babylonian period; the Aztecs and other peoples who inhabited the Basin of Mexico, in highland Mexico where Mexico City is now located, during the fifteenth and sixteenth centuries A.D.; the Mayas of southeastern Mexico, Belize, and parts of Guatemala and Honduras during the Classic Period between A.D. 200 and 900; and the Yorubas and neighboring Edo-speaking people of Benin in southwestern Nigeria during the eighteenth and nineteenth centuries A.D.

The urban centers of these states tended to be relatively large communities, with populations ranging from less than a thousand to over a hundred thousand individuals, depending on the ability of a particular city state to control and exact tribute from its neighbors. Considerable numbers of farmers frequently lived in such centers in order to secure greater protection for themselves and their possessions. It is estimated that in southern Mesopotamia in Early Dynastic times (ca. 2900–2350 B.C.) over 80 percent of the total population lived in urban centers (Adams 1981:90–94). Among the Yorubas, most extended families had their principal residences in towns and cities, although some members spent much of their lives in small villages or homesteads producing food for their relatives.

These cities also supported craft production, which sought to satisfy the demands not only of the urban elite but of society as a whole. The development of craft specialization and of commercial exchanges between town and countryside, as well as between neighboring urban centers, encouraged the growth of public markets. These were major features of urban life among the Aztecs and the Yorubas, and women in both cases played a prominent role in the retailing of goods. While the evidence for actual marketplaces is less clear for southern Mesopotamia, the remnants of shop-lined streets indicate vigorous commercial activity involving large numbers of people. This activity in turn promoted competition among city states to obtain supplies of exotic raw materials. As a result of widespread access to goods produced by full-time specialists and the development of more intensive agriculture close to urban centers, city states were able to support a considerable number of non-food producers, possibly 10 to 20 percent of the total population.

Other early civilizations formed large territorial states at an early stage in their development. Ancient Egypt, which consisted of the Nile Valley north of Aswan and its adjacent hinterland, was one of these. In the centuries prior to its unification, small states developed in southern Egypt and various parts of the north. Yet Egypt was politically united prior to the development of the court-centered tradition that was to characterize its elite culture from Early Dynastic times to the Late Period (Hoffman 1979). Another example is the Inka state, which arose in the central highlands of Peru in the fifteenth century A.D. This state originated in the region around Cuzco, in the central highlands of Peru, but by the time of the Spanish conquest embraced all the territory located west of the Amazonian rain forest from Ecuador to central Chile. While civilizations had developed earlier in the coastal and southern highland regions of Peru, there is no evidence of a major state having existed previously in what was to become the heartland of the Inka Empire (Keatinge 1988). Inka art and architecture were also different from those of any previous civilization in the region. A third example of a territorial state was centered in the eastern and central parts of the Yellow River valley of northern China during the Shang (ca. 1750– 1100 B.C.) and Western Chou (1100–771 B.C.) Dynasties and by the Western Chou period extended south to include parts of the Yangtze Valley. Although some scholars view northern China at this period as a network of city states, the evidence concerning the settlement patterns and administration of this region suggests two successive territorial states, although less powerful city and territorial states may have existed around their borders (Chang 1986b).

Territorial states developed a hierarchy of administrative centers at the local, provincial, and national levels, but these urban centers tended to have small populations. Even national capitals, with a maximum population of probably no more than fifty thousand people, were no larger than those of a substantial city state. This was because these centers were inhabited almost exclusively by the ruling class and by the administrators, craft specialists, and retainers who served them. Because of the security provided by the state, farmers tended to live in dispersed homesteads and in villages. The internal layout of administrative centers also tended to be decentralized. For this reason, Egypt was once characterized as a civilization without cities (Wilson 1960).

In territorial states a clearly demarcated two-tiered economy developed, with distinct rural and urban sectors. Farmers manufactured their own tools and household possessions on a part-time basis during periods of each year when they were not fully occupied with agricultural labor. Usually they utilized only locally-available raw materials and exchanged goods at local markets. Elite craftsmen, on the other hand, were employed by the state, either in provincial centers or at the national capital, to manufacture luxury goods for the king and the upper classes, often from raw materials imported specifically for that purpose. Unlike the city state, the only significant economic link between rural and urban centers in territorial states tended to be the payment of rents and taxes and the performance of corvées by peasants. The transfer of food surpluses from the countryside to urban centers took place principally in terms of appropriative rather than commercial mechanisms. Insofar as markets existed, they were usually small and served the needs of the local rural population and the urban poor.

Because of their large size, territorial states required large bureaucracies to ensure the collection of taxes that could be used to support state activities. Peasant communities, while becoming internally more hierarchical within the context of the state, tended to preserve more of their prestate culture than survived in city states, where large numbers of farmers came to reside in or near urban centers. Production was less specialized than it was in city states, full-time specialists fewer, and the quality of goods available to farmers poorer. Farming also appears to have been less intensive in territorial states, since there were fewer urban dwellers to feed. The percentage of the population not engaged in farming was probably less than 10 percent.

This suggests that, if a city-state civilization had become involved in prolonged conflict with a territorial state, despite the latter's

political unity, the greater technological and economic development of the city states would have given them a competitive edge.
This might help to explain why Egypt was relatively unsuccessful
when it engaged in military competition with the city-based states
of Southwest Asia, such as those of the Hittites and Assyrians. It
might also explain why at a later period the economically more
dynamic Greeks were able to resist and finally to conquer the
Persian Empire.

On the other hand, the government of a territorial state was able
to command the food surpluses and labor of a far greater number
of people than could the government of the largest city state. Hence
such governments were capable of undertaking projects on an
immense scale and could sponsor the work of many more skilled
craftsmen than could the elites of any city state. No buildings were
erected in southern Mesopotamia that remotely equaled in size or
engineering skill the pyramids at Giza, although during the Old
and Middle Kingdoms local temples in Egypt seem to have been
constructed on a more modest scale than were the temples in most
Mesopotamian cities. In the city states of Mexico, and especially
among the Mayas, elaborate stone architecture was common. It did
not equal, however, either in the scale of individual projects or in
the size of the stone blocks used, the monumental stone architecture that was erected over the very short life span of the Inka
empire.

The distinction between the political organization of city and
territorial states appears to be clear-cut rather than a matter of scale
or degree of integration. When city states conquered their neighbors, they normally compelled them to pay tribute but left their
political institutions and ruling families intact, preferring to rule
indirectly. Territorial states sometimes also controlled conquered
neighboring states in this manner, as New Kingdom Egypt did the
city states of Palestine and Syria. Inside the borders of territorial
states, however, local governments were dismantled and replaced
by a bureaucracy controlled by the central government. While local
people often continued to play a role in such administrations,
especially at the village level, no semi-autonomous state was permitted to threaten the control of the central government. Under
these circumstances, interstate tribute was replaced by intrastate

taxation as the basis for financing the activities of the central government. Just as the Egyptian kings molded the Nile Valley north of Aswan into a single state, the Inka rulers sought to convert the much larger Andean core, if not the whole, of their empire into a single state. The control that the central governments of these territorial states exerted was very different from the loose political hegemony and tribute payments that dominant Mesopotamian city states imposed on weaker ones, or that the Aztecs exerted over much of central Mexico.

The development of these two types of states might have been related to relative population densities at the time state formation occurred—territorial states perhaps emerging in areas of lower population density in relation to arable land. Lower population densities would have made it easier for defeated populations to seek refuge in more remote areas, which in turn would have inhibited the successful consolidation of any kind of state. In such areas power would have had to be based on control of larger regions. The Nile Valley north of Aswan was an area of overall low population density at the time of its first political unification (Butzer 1976). There is evidence that the pharaohs who established the First Dynasty not only ruled over the whole of the Nile Valley north of Aswan but also sought to enhance the natural borders of Egypt by depopulating adjacent areas of Nubia, the Sinai Peninsula, and probably Libya. This made it more difficult for Egyptians who objected to the authority of these pharaohs to avoid their rule (Hoffman 1979). However, too few data are available to test a general hypothesis concerning the relation between population density and the formation of different kinds of states. It is not encouraging that the Yorubas, who had a city-state system, also appear in recent times to have had a low absolute population density (Bascom 1955:452). Because of this, it is unrealistic to ignore the possibility that other important variables were involved.

It is significant that city and territorial states existed both in the Old World and the New World and that each type developed at various periods of human history. There is no evidence of historical relations between the different occurrences of the same kind of state; for example, territorial states such as Old Kingdom Egypt, Shang China, and Inka Peru or city-state networks such as ancient Mesopotamia, sixteenth-century Mexico, and eighteenth-century

Nigeria. Instead, these civilizations seem to provide evidence that two different types of political organization developed independently, at different periods, and in different parts of the world. Both types of civilization occurred along major rivers (Egypt, Shang China; Mesopotamia), in highland valleys (Peru; Mexico), and perhaps, if we include the Khmer state of Cambodia as an example of a territorial state (Higham 1989), in tropical forests as well (Maya, Yoruba; Khmer). Nor is literacy associated exclusively with one sort of state. Among territorial states Egypt and China developed literacy, the Inkas did not; among city states the Mesopotamians and the Mayas achieved literacy, while the Aztecs and other highland Mexicans remained semi-literate, and the Yorubas did not develop writing.

The development under these varied circumstances of only two basic types of political organization suggests that there may be only a limited number of viable ways in which societies at any particular level of complexity can be organized (Murdock 1959:134), a possibility further indicated by the recent collapse, after a relatively brief duration, of the Soviet variant of industrialized society (Harris 1992). I believe that these limitations at the political level are likely to be explained in terms of varying costs of decision-making and political control in different kinds of societies. (Flannery 1972; Johnson 1973; Adams 1988; Tainter 1988).

Comparative Studies

During the past four decades anthropological archaeologists have spent much time studying how early civilizations developed (Adams 1966; R.E.W. Adams 1977; Redman 1978; Hoffman 1979; Jones and Kautz 1981). Since archaeology's chief strength is what it can reveal about changes over long periods of time, this seems to be a potentially highly productive approach. However, while these efforts have resulted in major discoveries relating to the development of specific early civilizations, the theoretical advances do not seem proportional to the amount of energy expended. There are at least two main reasons for this.

First, the origins of early civilizations everywhere predated the earliest appearance of substantial written records. Yet there is much we need to know about the early development of civilizations that we cannot reasonably hope to learn from archaeological data alone. One needs only to think of the controversies concerning the nature of the social and political organization of the Indus Valley civilization that remain unresolved for lack of contemporary written records. Second, as a result of prolonged occupation, the earliest levels at many important sites have been buried under thick layers of debris from later periods. Because of this, archaeologists are limited in what they can learn about the formative stages of civilization at many key centers. It will take a long time to uncover crucial archaeological evidence concerning the initial development of many early civilizations.

For these reasons I thought it worthwhile to attempt a comparative study of periods of early civilizations that are well documented both archaeologically and textually. My ultimate goal was to learn more about the factors that constrain human behavior by examining the similarities and differences in the ways in which a significant number of civilizations that had evolved independently, or almost independently, in different parts of the world had been structured and how each of them had functioned.

Some archaeologists and anthropologists question the validity of any kind of comparative study. Especially among anthropologists who have adopted a structuralist viewpoint, there has been a revival of the Boasian position that every culture is unique and that, while each one can be studied and understood on its own terms, individual cultures cannot legitimately be compared with one another. This position has been adopted with respect to the Inkas by many Andeanists. They view Inka civilization as the expression of a unique set of beliefs that are of great antiquity in the Central Andes and which made, and continue to make, Inka culture fundamentally different from any other (D'Altroy 1987:5). More generally, Ian Hodder (1986, 1987b) has argued that, because each culture is the product of its own history, cross-cultural comparison is impossible. It is not clear how forcefully Hodder holds this view, since this claim has not prevented him from proposing various cross-cultural generalizations of his own (Hodder 1982:67).

These historical particularist views reflect the belief that what Marshall Sahlins (1976) calls "cultural reason," by which he means decision-making constrained by the idiosyncratic values of specific cultural traditions, plays a greater role in determining human behavior than does "practical reason," the universally comprehensible calculation of the material interests of individuals and groups. My own view, when beginning this study, was that the extent of idiosyncrasies and of cross-cultural regularities was something that archaeologists and anthropologists had to determine empirically. Nevertheless, I also accepted that previous cross-cultural studies had indicated enough regularities among societies to suggest that such investigations were both possible and interesting.

Social anthropologists have long objected to the cross-cultural comparison of individual traits wrenched from their sociopolitical context (Harris 1968:612–33; Köbben 1952, 1973). While I accept that there is much validity in this criticism, I nevertheless continue to value this form of cross-cultural comparison as a useful tool for exploring general propositions about relations between different aspects of culture (Moore 1961; Ford 1967; Jorgensen 1974; Murdock 1981). The more serious problem is that most of the more robust correlations tend to be self-evident. It is no great surprise to learn that no hunter–gatherer culture has a divine kingship. On the other hand, most other correlations tend to be ambiguous 'tendencies' and 'tilts,' which suggests that multiple factors are involved whose interrelations can be understood only through more detailed study of individual cases (Coult and Habenstein 1965; Textor 1967). Only rarely do robust correlations emerge that are not self-evident (Betzig 1986).

To avoid the problems inherent in non-contextualized trait comparisons, I decided to conduct a detailed study of seven early civilizations located in different parts of the world. I hoped that this selection was large enough to constitute a reasonable sample of the basic similarities and differences found in all early civilizations and small enough so that I could understand each civilization in structural and functional terms before I attempted a cross-cultural comparison. In this way I sought to answer the social and structural anthropologists' objection that cross-cultural studies cannot produce useful results because they compare traits in isolation from the functional and historical contexts which endow them with behavioral significance. In presenting the results of a comparative study, data must necessarily be isolated from their social context. Prior to my eventual publication of summary descriptions of each civilization, readers will have to accept on trust that I attempted a reasonable contextual analysis.

I am surprised by how little importance archaeologists ascribe to this more rigorous form of comparison. Despite Lewis Binford's (1972) demands for theoretical rigor in delineating regularities in human behavior, a cross-cultural generalization about hunter–gatherers consists of a pattern he has observed among the Nunamiut Eskimos of Alaska that is not contradicted by sometimes casual observations that he and other anthropologists have made among the San (Bushmen) of South Africa and the Australian aborigines. The slightest evidence of regularity is accepted as indicating that certain forms of behavior characterize hunter–gatherer life everywhere (Binford 1983:144–92). This is very different from attempting a systematic comparison of hunter–gatherer cultures in different parts of the world.

Nor is any effort made to determine whether hunter–gatherer life has been modified by contacts with Europeans in recent centuries (Binford 1980). To what extent do similarities in hunter–gatherer life in Siberia and North America result from age-old patterns of adaptation to the natural environment or from a far more recent adaptation to the fur trade? In general, scholars tend to be highly critical of evidence that contradicts what they want to believe, while easily accepting what supports their presuppositions. In this instance, neoevolutionary faith in the uniformity of human behavior seems to encourage a belief that what holds true for one or two groups of hunter–gatherers, or any other type of society, is likely to hold true for all of them.

Methodology

From the available literature I have tried to compile for each civilization as much information as I can concerning the environment, population density and distribution, technology, subsistence patterns, trade, manufacture and distribution of goods, family and community organization, religious beliefs and practices, legal systems, moral codes, art, and concepts about the nature of the individual and of desirable forms of behavior. My aim in each case has been to ascertain how these elements constituted a way of life in individual civilizations before attempting cross-cultural comparisons.

The amount of research that I do concerning each civilization is determined empirically, by noting when I start to encounter a marked and consistent decline in new information. I have found that this tends to occur after I have read thirty to fifty recent scholarly books dealing with each civilization. I then add recently published studies only if they elucidate a significant aspect of an early civilization that has not yet been covered. Securing adequate coverage of the literature is not an easy task. My comparison is not yet finished and my conclusions therefore remain tentative.

To limit imposing my own preconceptions on the data, I have tried as much as possible to understand each civilization as it was perceived by the people who lived in it; that is, from what social anthropologists would call an 'emic' perspective. I have done this by noting the terms used in each civilization for such items as social classes, administrative titles, categories of landholding, and supernatural beings. Only for ancient Egypt do I have even the rudimentary language skills required to do this systematically. Yet, even when depending solely upon glosses in secondary sources, I have found this approach helpful.

This is because words do not always mean what their English translations imply. The Aztecs had two terms that are often translated as 'peasant.' The first of these, *macehualli*, referred to a taxpaying member of a collective landowning group and the second, *mayeque*, to a rent-paying individual bound to land owned or held in return for service to the state by a member of the nobility. The word for king is also used differently in various early civilizations. The Aztec word *tlatoani*, meaning 'great speaker,' was applied to the ruler of every duly constituted city state, just as the English term 'king' refers to the ruler of any kingdom. Yet the ancient Egyptian word for king, *nsw*, was never applied to foreign rulers, who were designated *ḥḳ3* ('ruler') or *wr* ('prince'). It has long been recognized that words that are glossed as 'slave' have notoriously different meanings from one society to another (Watson 1980).

Terms referring to the supernatural can be particularly misleading. According to Jan Assmann, ancient Egyptian concepts of time cannot be understood without knowing that they had two words for 'eternity,' *nḥḥ* and *ḏt*, which did not mean the same thing; *nḥḥ* referring to eternal cycles of recurrence and *ḏt* to eternal changelessness. Neither of these words referred to eternity as we understand it, but instead to a length of time corresponding to the duration of the existing cosmic order (Allen 1988:25–27). The Aztecs ascribed to each human being at least three 'souls' or 'life forces': the *tonalli*, associated with the head, which was a source of strength, vigor, and rationality, and which could be reborn in one's descendants; the *teyoli*, associated with the heart and personality, which eventually went to the realms of the dead; and the *ihiyotl*, associated with the liver and with emotion. In life the Aztecs sought to maintain a harmonious relation among these forces, although such an integration could not last beyond death (López Austin 1988:253). This reminds us of Egyptian soul concepts, such as *b3*, *k3*, and *3h̠*, whose precise significance is the subject of continuing debate (Baines 1991:145). It also calls to mind the possible complexities of meaning that may underlie poorly understood religious concepts in other civilizations. As a result of ignorance, it is all too easy to impose our own concepts on other peoples. Hence for each civilization I have attempted to determine as much as I can about how they conceptualized their world before attempting to 'translate' such concepts into a 'scientific,' cross-culturally applicable terminology. Where this exercise does not produce enlightenment, because the original terminology is not systematically preserved or is inadequately understood, it at least helps to reveal the limitations of the current understanding of a particular civilization.

I have sought to examine the earliest phase of civilization in each region for which there is not only good archaeological evidence but also substantial written records that shed light on aspects of human behavior and belief that cannot be ascertained from material culture alone. These written records were produced either by the literate elements in the society being studied or by European visitors and colonists. A third, non-archaeological, kind of data consists of oral traditions and memories of indigenous customs that were recorded by or from native people after European contact. My requirement of substantial written sources means that I never study the earliest stage in the development of civilization in each area. This is especially the case with civilizations that did not develop their own writing systems. Such civilizations had flourished in the Basin of Mexico for over fifteen hundred years prior to the Late Aztec period and in parts of

Peru for an equal time prior to the arrival of the Spanish (Sanders, Parsons, and Santley 1979; Keatinge 1988). We also know from archaeological evidence that at least some Yoruba states, as well as Benin, had existed for many centuries prior to the arrival of European traders and missionaries in West Africa and before the Yorubas learned to write as a result of European contact (Shaw 1978; Connah 1987).

On the other hand, we have information about earlier stages of literate civilizations. These include Old and Middle Kingdom Egypt, Mesopotamia from the Early Dynastic III (ca. 2600 B.C.) period onward, and Chinese civilization beginning in the late Shang Dynasty. After my research had begun, I added the Classic Maya civilization, which, as a result of recent successes in deciphering its hieroglyphic inscriptions, has joined the ranks of early civilizations whose scripts can be read. This was especially desirable as it added another tropical forest civilization to my sample. I would have liked to include at least one early civilization from the Indian subcontinent, but not enough information was available concerning the Indus and Gangetic civilizations to justify adding either of them to my sample. The same was true for the Khmer civilization of Southeast Asia. Probably the most detailed record, both archaeological and literary, of life at a single point in time in any early civilization is that for the Aztecs during the early sixteenth century. Following the Spanish conquest, Spanish priests and native Mexicans recorded an extraordinary wealth of information concerning traditional Aztec culture.

While the Mayas and Aztecs are historically and culturally, although not linguistically, related, I judged that adding the Mayas did not compromise my sample, which is not a statistical one. The very different environmental settings and different economic and political organizations of these two groups were reasons for including both. Nor is there evidence that the other civilizations are similar mainly as a result of historical contacts. Ancient Egypt and Mesopotamia communicated with each other at various periods and both clearly emerged from a Neolithic ecumene that extended over much of North Africa and the Middle East (Frankfort 1956). The development of Chinese civilization may have been influenced to some degree by indirect contacts with the civilizations of Western Asia (Chang 1962) and there were limited contacts between Mexico and Peru at various periods (Hosler 1988). On the other hand, there are unlikely to have been any significant contacts between China and the New World after human groups spread from Siberia into North America sometime before 12,000 B.C. Yet, if the religions of the Aztecs, Mayas, and the Shang Dynasty are all derived from historically-related shamanistic cults dating back to the Palaeolithic period, this might account for certain similarities among all three (Willey 1985). While I do not rule out historical connections among various civilizations, the fact that ancient Egypt and Mesopotamia, which were separated by only a few hundred kilometers and grew out of historically-related Neolithic cultures, were so different indicates that the seven cases I am studying can be treated as essentially independent examples of early civilizations. Each represents a stage in the cultural development of a region that conforms to my definition of an early civilization. That seems to be more important for determining how representative my sample is of the various types of early civilizations than whether or not these societies are totally pristine or represent the earliest phase in the development of civilization in each region.

My original aim was to examine each society as a way of life that had existed at a specific point in time, thereby treating it in a manner approximating the traditional anthropological concept of the 'ethnographic present.' In this fashion I hoped to avoid conflating practices that might have existed at different periods in a single society's development. In practice, however, I did not find it possible, even as an analytical fiction, to limit my studies to a single point in time, nor do I now believe that it would have been a good idea to have tried to do so. I accept Evans-Pritchard's (1962) argument that the best way to learn how the parts of a culture fit together is to observe how they change in relation to one another. My findings so far suggest that this is particularly useful for understanding political organization, since bureaucratic structures often change rapidly as members of the governing hierarchy seek to alter such relations to their own advantage. Hence when I examine ancient Egypt I consider both the Old and Middle Kingdoms, and in some cases use New Kingdom literary texts to illuminate aspects of life that were not recorded earlier. I try, however, to exclude the major sociopolitical changes that occurred in Egyptian society after the end of the Middle Kingdom. Likewise for Mesopotamia, I consider data from the earliest appearance of readable texts in the Early Dynastic III period to the lasting unification of the region during the Old Babylonian Period (ca. 1750 B.C.) and for China from the Shang Dynasty to the end of the Western Chou. While acknowledging that major economic, political, and social changes occurred in these civilizations over such a long time, I believe that the available evidence illustrates a particular kind of society that had many features in common and was significantly different from what existed both earlier and later. For the Mayas the period of substantial written documentation covers approximately six hundred years, while for the Aztecs, Inkas, and Yorubas it spans only one to two hundred years. In each of these cultures, these were times of major social change.

Sources

There are numerous problems with data in a study of this sort. While archaeological findings are far from uniform, they provide the information that is most comparable from one early civilization to another. By far the best archaeological data come from the settlement pattern surveys that have been carried out in southern Iraq (Adams 1981), the Basin of Mexico (Sanders, Parsons, and Santley 1979), and in recent years over large stretches of Maya territory (Culbert and Rice 1990). While much has been learned about the settlement patterns of ancient Egypt, the data base remains less comprehensive (Butzer 1976). Still less is known archaeologically about settlement patterns in Shang China (Wheatley 1971; Chang 1980) and Inka Peru (Hyslop 1990). Despite these shortcomings, archaeological data, in their concreteness, provide much information about daily life in early civilizations. They are also data which, while they may have been biased by regional patterns of archaeological research, are unlikely to have been deliberately distorted by the people who produced them.

Written sources, on the other hand, while essential for understanding many aspects of life, rarely provide unbiased information. The records produced by early civilizations, either in the form of indigenous writings or of oral traditions recorded under various colonial regimes, tend to reflect the preoccupations and interests of officials and the upper classes. It is also increasingly being appreciated to what a great extent indigenous peoples modified their oral traditions to adapt them to colonial situations (Gillespie 1989, Apter 1992:193–211). In particular, the native elites who survived into the colonial period were anxious to promote an image of their traditional culture, and especially of their personal ancestors, that would win the approval of influential Europeans. Histories were also revised as a way to cope with national defeat and humiliation. The records produced by colonists reflected to no less a degree the issues that interested them. In particular, these included indigenous patterns of land ownership and tribute payments, in order to facilitate acquiring control over local resources; and religious beliefs, in order to assist Christian missionaries in stamping out traditional religions (Durán 1971:34–35).

Interpretations

Modern interpretations of early civilizations are also markedly biased. Understanding and making allowances for these biases is vital for the success of any investigation that depends mostly on secondary sources. Anthropological interests in the early civilizations have changed significantly in recent decades, as anthropology has shifted its principal focus from a concern with social behavior to a renewed interest in culture. Studies of the early civilizations produced in the 1960s were dominated by a materialistic perspective that encouraged an interest in subsistence patterns, craft production, exchange, settlement patterns, and to a lesser degree political organization as the most important factors shaping human life. Today there is an escalating interest in religious beliefs and culturally determined perceptions, both for their own sake and as major determinants of social and political behavior. While the idealist perspective that underlies much modern research is clearly at odds with the materialism of an earlier era, the research of these two periods tends to be complementary and, when combined, produces richer and more nuanced insights into the nature of earlier civilizations than the literature of either period does by itself.

Other biases color studies either of individual early civilizations or of all of them, the latter sort creating the more serious problems of comparability for cross-cultural investigations. Interpreters of

Aztec culture have long been divided between those who view the Aztec elite as cynical imperialists or bloodthirsty cannibals (Caso 1958; Soustelle 1961) and those who see them as philosophers seeking to understand the mysteries of life (León-Portilla 1963, 1992). Inka studies have been dominated in recent decades by the assumption that the Inka state was constructed by utilizing the expectations of reciprocal aid that were deeply rooted in the traditions of Central Andean peasant life to validate the increasingly asymmetrical relations between different classes (Masuda, Shimada, and Morris 1985). These studies read very differently from Thomas Patterson's (1991) investigation of Inka dynastic politics, which places a heavy emphasis on the practice of realpolitik among the various branches of the royal family and their supporters.

The interpretation of ancient Mesopotamian civilization has been heavily influenced by that civilization's historical connections with the Old Testament, which have stimulated scholars to seek in it the origins of Western civilization. That in turn has led them to interpret their data in ways that probably make Mesopotamia appear more like modern Western civilization than was actually the case, and hence exaggerate the differences between it and other early civilizations (Bottéro 1992).

Two Dutch social anthropologists, Thomas Zuidema (1964, 1990) and Rudolph van Zantwijk (1985), have presented extremely elaborate structural analyses of Inka and Aztec religious beliefs. Of these studies one can state, as Barry Kemp (1989:4–5) has about some of the more arcane interpretations of ancient Egyptian symbolism, that, while their constructions may "be quite true to the spirit of ancient thought," we have no way of determining whether such ideas "ever actually passed through the minds of the ancients."

The study of ancient Egypt has long been dominated by the rationalist belief that all human beings share a nature that is similar to our own and that this similarity makes the ancients immediately comprehensible to modern scholars. Most Egyptologists I have known seem convinced that they can duplicate in their own minds the thought processes of a Hatshepsut, Akhenaton, or Ramesses II. As a result of this pervasive uniformitarianism, Egyptology has never produced a work of critical theoretical insight comparable to Leo Oppenheim's *Ancient Mesopotamia* (1964). This rationalist approach is the opposite of the romantic anthropological assumption held by Inka specialists, many of whom believe that human nature is powerfully molded by individual cultures and that hence, without paying careful attention to the idiosyncratic postulates of Inka culture, it is wholly impossible to understand Inka behavior. Although Barry Kemp, who has discussed these theoretical issues in detail, agrees with Henri Frankfort (1956) that certain distinctive themes shaped Egyptian culture, even he interprets much ancient Egyptian behavior as being influenced by concepts of self-interest and entrepreneurship that he considers common to all human beings.

Finally, I must stress that each of the early civilizations I am studying was a complex institution that endured over many generations and embraced millions of human beings, each of whom thought her or his own thoughts and lived her or his own life. Even those who study the best-documented early civilizations are in the position of the proverbial blind men trying to comprehend an elephant. There is much that is important about every early civilization that we do not know and that in some instances we may never be able to learn. Moreover, what we do know about one early civilization is often radically different from what we know about another. One of the chief benefits of comparative study is that knowledge of one early civilization may reveal gaps in our knowledge of others and stimulate research that helps to fill these gaps. For example, the striking archaeological successes achieved in studying the settlement patterns of southern Iraq and the Basin of Mexico have challenged Egyptologists to seek more comprehensive information about ancient Egyptian settlement patterns.

Conclusion

In the chapters that follow I will not be able to describe in detail each of the early civilizations that I have been studying. I will try, however, to ascertain some of the ways in which ancient Egypt resembled other early civilizations and some of the ways in which it was unique. Cross-cultural parallels may provide Egyptologists with new insights into the nature of ancient Egyptian civilization, while those aspects that are unique to Egypt may help anthropologists to understand better the nature of early civilizations and of humanity as a whole. No doubt Egyptologists will consider some of my generalizations about ancient Egypt to be premature, questionable, or even plain wrong. There is little about ancient Egypt, or any other early civilization, that is not subject to debate among specialists. I ask Egyptologists to treat my statements not as evidence of the uselessness of what I am attempting but as a challenge to debate issues that are significant not only for their discipline but for the general understanding of early civilizations. When it comes to the study of ancient Egypt, Egyptologists and anthropologists have much to learn from each other, and their different orientations are a potential source of mutual benefit. Rather than trying to turn Egyptologists into anthropologists or anthropologists into Egyptologists, I suggest that specialists in either discipline can best help each other by continuing to do what they have learned to do best.

Two

Economic Foundations

Compared with some other early civilizations, relatively little attention has been paid to how the economy of ancient Egypt functioned. The main reason for this is the lack of large numbers of economic texts, such as those that are available for Mesopotamia and to a much lesser extent for the Aztecs. The famous letters of the Eleventh Dynasty mortuary priest, Hekanakhte, reveal a tight-fisted and irascible official who rented extra land, lent substantial amounts of grain, and had at his disposal surplus copper, oil, and cloth woven from flax grown on his estate, all of which he used for commercial transactions. To the members of his household, including his mother, he issued monthly food rations in the same manner as was done to workmen employed on state projects (James 1962). At the level of human interaction, these letters are sufficiently detailed that they inspired Agatha Christie's novel *Death Comes as the End*.

Yet we cannot learn from these letters such basic facts as on what terms Hekanakhte held his estate at Nebeseyet or whether the men of his household were really his sons, or merely tenants. The same holds true for most other ancient Egyptian economic texts. Only for a small number, such as the ones from the New Kingdom tomb workers' village at Deir al-Medina (Bierbrier 1982), are adequate contextual data available. A comparative perspective is useful for gaining insights into topics about which relatively little is known. I hope that Egyptologists may draw from the following discussion a broader awareness of economic issues that are worth addressing with respect to ancient Egypt.

27

When I began my research I assumed, like many other anthropologists, that aspects of early civilizations that were shaped most directly by the constraints of environment and technology would display the greatest degree of cross-cultural uniformity. Even at this level there were problems. Anthropologists had long rejected any simplistic form of technological determinism. All the early civilizations practiced metallurgy. Yet, throughout the long history of civilization among the Mayas and in the Basin of Mexico, metalworking was employed only to produce ornaments. The Inkas, Shang Chinese, and Old and Middle Kingdom Egyptians also manufactured copper and bronze weapons and tools for skilled craftsmen, but few, if any, agricultural implements. Only the early Mesopotamians produced a broader range of tools for everyday use. In West Africa, the large-scale working of iron preceded the rise of Yoruba civilization. Because of these variations, it had been concluded that the main economic factor shaping the development of early civilizations was more intensive food production, in relation to which cutting-tool technologies played only a minor role.

In accord with my belief that the early civilizations had been shaped most directly by economic factors, I also assumed that one would encounter more cross-cultural diversity in social and political institutions, because these were less directly constrained by environment and technology, and still more diversity in art, philosophy, and religious beliefs, which were the aspects of behavior most likely to be influenced by historical idiosyncrasies (Friedman and Rowlands 1978:203–5; Gellner 1982). This, however, is not what I have found.

Agriculture

First I discovered that there is a wide range of variation among the early civilizations in terms of ecological adaptations. Some had dense populations supported by intensive multicropping. The most spectacular example of this was found in the southern part of the Basin of Mexico in the Late Aztec period. There large areas of permanent irrigation and of chinampas produced as many as four crops each year. Chinampas were fields created by piling up soil to raise it above water levels in swamps and shallow lakes. This normally produced a pattern of long, narrow fields, which could be watered by hand and have their soil renewed with silt that collected in the intervening canals and ditches. Even within their capital city, Tenochtitlan, which was built on islands near the shore of a network of lakes in the center of the valley, the Aztecs practiced chinampa agriculture on small fields behind their homes. These fields were fertilized with household organic waste. The main chinampas that fed Tenochtitlan were located in the shallow lakes to the west and south of the city. By building an extensive series of dikes, the Aztecs succeeded in regulating lake levels and reducing salinity in those areas. It is calculated that about 120 square kilometers of chinampas had been constructed by 1519. At that time, the Basin of Mexico is estimated to have had an overall population density of about 200 people per square kilometer and as many as 500 persons per square kilometer of arable land (Sanders, Parsons, and Santley 1979:219, 378–80).

The Mayas, who lived in the tropical forests of southern Mexico and Central America, had a relatively dispersed settlement pattern. Even in urban centers, this left much room for gardening around their individual residential compounds. These gardens, like the small ones adjacent to Aztec homes, were no doubt heavily fertilized with household waste and multicropped. Outside the urban centers, where the terrain was suitable, the Mayas developed chinampas and irrigated fields, which they multicropped, as well as terraced hillsides. They also continued to practice less labor-intensive slash-and-burn agriculture. They are estimated to have maintained over large areas a population density that averaged 180 people per square kilometer, comparing favorably with that of preindustrial Java and China (Culbert and Rice 1990:26). Neither the Aztecs nor the Mayas had any large domestic animals. They kept dogs and turkeys, both of which they ate.

In other early civilizations, only one crop was grown each year on most fields and part of the terrain was used for grazing. Most peasant villages in the Central Andes were located between 2500 and 3500 meters above sea level. The villagers grew corn in the valleys below and potatoes on the colder slopes above. On the still higher uplands, they pastured camel-like llamas and alpacas which provided them with wool and meat. Because of the steep slopes and irregular rainfall, these communities frequently constructed extensive terraces, which they irrigated with runoff. They also established small colonies at lower altitudes to plant chili, cotton, and other crops that would not grow on the mountainsides.

The Mesopotamians, living in a desert environment, constructed elaborate irrigation works on the broad, gentle backslopes of the levees that flanked the lower stretches of their main rivers. Although the lower part of the Euphrates River was at that time divided into several branches, it and the Tigris were hard to control. Both rivers were at their lowest when crops had to be planted in the autumn and in flood when they were ripening in the spring. This required barriers to prevent the destruction of crops. Other major problems were salinization, loss of soil fertility, and disposal of surplus water. For all these reasons, considerable engineering and agronomic skills were required to construct and maintain even the medium-sized irrigation systems that were utilized prior to the late first millennium B.C. Multicropping and date-growing tended to be limited to gardens located along the tops of levees, while the backslopes were used to grow barley and wheat. Fields left in fallow, marshland, and steppe land that received sufficient winter rains were used to graze cattle, sheep, and goats. The main grazing lands were located between and beyond the areas of irrigation agriculture. Robert McC. Adams (1981:90, 148–49) has estimated a population density of only thirty people per square kilometer of arable land during the Ur III Period, and a total population for southern Mesopotamia at that time of about 500, 000.

Prior to the Ptolemaic era, the Egyptians generally grew only one crop per year, except in kitchen gardens which were watered by hand or with shadufs. The Nile floods were, however, more predictable than those of the Tigris and Euphrates and subsided before the late autumn when wheat, barley, and other crops were planted. Because the river sank below the level of the floodplain during the summer, the soil also tended to be self-rinsing and salinization was not a major problem. The basin agriculture practiced by the Egyptians utilized abandoned natural levees running parallel to the course of the river. These were reinforced with lateral embankments and supplied with irrigation ditches to control the entry and exit of flood waters. In this way, it was ensured that even land located on high ground in relation to the river was covered by water long enough to produce a crop. These systems were easier to construct and maintain than were the Mesopotamian irrigation works, especially in the far south of Egypt, where the natural basins were smaller than they were in central Egypt and the Delta. It used to be believed that annual deposits of Nile silt maintained the fertility of the fields, but it is now clear that this involved crop rotation, fallowing, and pasturing cattle on the stubble so that their manure fertilized the soil, as that of wild herbivores had done prior to the development of agriculture. It appears that pastoralism was essential to sustain the Egyptian agricultural cycle (Hunt 1987). Karl Butzer's (1976:83) population estimates of 1.2 million people for the Old Kingdom and 2 million for the Middle Kingdom yield population densities of only 93 and 108 persons per square kilometer of arable land. Even if we were to allow a population as high as 3 million, which I do not consider unreasonable, the population density would have been only 176 people per square kilometer, far short of the 500 people per square kilometer estimated for arable land in the Basin of Mexico.

Little is known about agriculture in Shang China. It was based on growing sorghum, millet, and other crops on easily worked loess soils relying mainly on rainfall, and on domestic animals. Hence it probably supported a relatively low population density. The simplest subsistence economy associated with an early civilization was that of the Yorubas. Large numbers of Yorubas lived in urban centers, but fields extended far from these towns and often were worked by family members who resided part-time or full-time in scattered homesteads and hamlets. Farms were sufficiently dispersed to allow families to rotate fields as the soil became exhausted, observing a seven to twenty year fallow, without having to move their houses. Although fields and forests were sometimes located between the inner and outer walls that surrounded Yoruba towns, and although land close to towns and cities seems to have been worked more intensively than land farther away, there was no intensive 'infield' cultivation around Yoruba urban residences, as was the case with the Mayas and the Aztecs. Data from recent times suggest an overall population density of only thirty to sixty people per square kilometer for the Yoruba and Benin kingdoms (Bascom 1969:2; Eades 1980:2; Bradbury 1957:14).

The origin of civilization has often been attributed to increasing population pressure within naturally circumscribed areas (Cohen

1977). The population of the Basin of Mexico was perhaps close to the sustaining capacity of its environment, which may have been one reason why the Aztecs had begun to establish colonies in other parts of their empire. It has also been suggested that by Late Classic times the Maya population density had reached the point where it was inflicting serious damage on the natural environment. Yet civilization had begun in both regions when the population density had been much lower than it was in the Late Aztec and Late Classic Maya periods, and agricultural production had been less intensive.

By contrast, the ancient Egyptian state throughout its history pursued a policy of settling large numbers of captives and immigrants in various parts of the country. In early times, such extra labor may have played a significant role in developing new estates, especially in the Delta region. By increasing the number of their subjects, Egyptian rulers sought to increase their own wealth. It is also likely that the settlement of immigrants, especially Semitic-speaking pastoralists, may have been of demographic importance in Mesopotamia. There, because of medical problems resulting from crowded living conditions, urban populations—which in the Early Dynastic Period included most of the population—may have been unable to reproduce themselves (McNeill 1976). It is worth considering whether their predominantly urban lifestyle might account for the gradual disappearance of Sumerian speakers. It is also significant that the Ibos of Eastern Nigeria did not develop cities or states, although their overall population was about the same as that of the Yorubas and their population density approximately twice as high (Bascom 1955:452). Consequently, population density and population pressure cannot be considered major independent variables that by themselves account for the development of civilizations.

On the other hand, the development of urbanism appears to have been a significant factor stimulating more intensive agriculture in areas adjacent to cities in order to minimize transportation costs (Netting 1969). For ecological and political reasons, this process seems to have been carried further by the Aztecs, who had developed an extremely populous hegemonic city state, than it was by the Mesopotamians, Mayas, or Yorubas.

In general, investment in hydraulic works and terracing correlated with the intensity of crop production. The creation of this infrastructure also required the development of organizational skills. Most of the labor needed to construct and maintain irrigation works, terraces, and chinampas could be organized at the village or district level, although the big diking projects carried out by the Aztecs and some of the major terracing done by the Inkas were state projects, as was the agricultural development of the Fayyum in Middle Kingdom Egypt. In most of the early civilizations planting and harvesting seem to have been accomplished collectively or on a labor-swapping basis by teams of relatives or neighbors, although the crops harvested from specific plots of land belonged to single families or individuals. These forms of cooperation must have provided a model for organizing larger village and district projects. The once popular idea that the need for larger irrigation systems resulted in despotic state control at an early stage in the development of civilization (Steward 1949) failed to appreciate the small-scale and piecemeal nature of most hydraulic works in the early civilizations. Large, state-managed irrigation systems appear to have been a product of the state rather than the reverse (Adams 1965).

Agricultural tools generally remained primitive in the early civilizations. The Inkas, Aztecs, and Shang Chinese relied on wooden digging sticks equipped with foot-bars to turn the soil, while their cutting tools were made of stone. The Mesopotamians and Egyptians employed light, oxen-drawn plows to conserve soil moisture and prepare the soil for planting; Mesopotamian plows were also equipped with drills to plant seed. While the Mesopotamians began to use copper hoes and sickles during the Early Dynastic Period, as late as the Middle Kingdom the Egyptians continued to edge their cutting tools with chipped flint. The Yorubas had no use for plows in connection with their slash-and-burn agriculture, but they equipped their hoes and other agricultural tools with iron blades. The complexity of the tools available in each early civilization does not correlate with the intensity of agricultural production; nor do any of these civilizations appear to have had tools as elaborate as those possessed by the tribal societies of Iron Age Europe. This suggests that there is no close correlation between types of agricultural tools and either the intensity of agricultural production or the complexity of society.

There is also no evident correlation between the intensity of agriculture and the general nature of the environment. The least intensive system in my sample was that of the Yorubas, who inhabited a tropical forest and savannah environment. But the Mayas, who also lived in tropical forests, used a combination of chinampas, irrigation, terracing, and slash-and-burn agriculture to support a higher population density than appears to have been achieved in Egypt and Mesopotamia. There is no support for Julian Steward's (1949) claim that early civilizations came into existence only as a consequence of the development of water management in semi-arid environments. Furthermore, the civilizations that developed in highland Mexico and Peru were institutionally as complex and varied as those in the much larger river valleys of Egypt, Mesopotamia, and northern China.

Finally, there is no clear correlation between intensity of agriculture and the architectural achievements of these early civilizations. The smallest amount of monumental architecture has survived from the Yoruba and ancient Chinese civilizations, which had two of the least intensive subsistence economies. There is no evidence, however, that the highly efficient subsistence systems practiced in the Basin of Mexico resulted in more monumental architecture throughout that region than was produced by the Mayas, Egyptians, and Mesopotamians. In Chapter Three, I will demonstrate that, while agricultural surpluses are needed to produce monumental architecture, the extent and nature of such architecture are determined primarily by political and religious factors.

Kinship

In the early civilizations, kinship tended to remain important within each class, although specific kinship arrangements varied considerably from one civilization to another. There were also differences among classes within the same civilization, with the upper classes generally placing greater emphasis on tracking genealogies and having more generations of the same family living together than was the case for peasant families.

Yoruba society was based on patrilineal descent. Especially in the northern regions of Yoruba territory, large numbers of kin related in the male line lived together in one or more self-governing extended family compounds. While personally-acquired property was inherited by daughters as well as by sons, lineage property had to pass to a man's sons or, if he had none, to his younger brothers. In order to protect their patrilineal landholding patterns, Yoruba spouses were forbidden to inherit from one another.

The Aztecs and the Inkas lived in nuclear or small extended families. The Aztecs emphasized patrilineal descent, but also derived significant social status from their mothers' families. Both sons and daughters inherited property from their parents, and household utensils usually passed to a woman's daughters. The Inkas appear to have practiced double descent, which involved women inheriting goods and offices from their mothers and men from their fathers. Both Aztec and Inka peasants were members of endogamous landowning groups. This arrangement minimized the dangers of the group losing property through inheritance.

The Mesopotamians emphasized patrilineal descent and at least some extended families appear to have possessed various rights in common. Women could inherit property, but in wealthy families this right was often curtailed by having some female members join celibate religious organizations in order to ensure that their property would eventually return to their families.

The ancient Egyptian expression for marriage, *grg-pr*, 'to found a house,' suggests that a nuclear family residence was an ideal, although among wealthy families, such as that of Hekanakhte, several generations of adults seem to have lived under a single roof. Egyptians were frequently identified by citing their father's or mother's name as well as their own, and in the Late Period some individuals are reported to have possessed genealogies that extended back over many generations. Yet they did not recognize any formally constituted descent groups.

The Egyptians are notable for not having any primary kin terms other than those which applied to the nuclear family; they had no special words for aunt, uncle, niece, nephew, cousin, or even for grandparents and grandchildren (O'Connor 1990). The extremely abbreviated kinship terminology of the Egyptians, with its specific terms covering only three generations, contrasts with the seven-generational one of the Aztecs. In the New Kingdom even the words for husband (*hy*) and wife (*ḥmt*) tended to be replaced by those used for brother (*sn*) and sister (*snt*), a usage that left brother and sister the only terms for that generation and in modern times has given rise to much groundless speculation about the extent of brother–sister marriage outside the royal family. The extended use that the Egyptians made of their kin terms suggests little interest in distinguishing between immediate and more remote ancestors or descendants, or between maternal and paternal relatives. At most, an attempt was made to distinguish between direct and collateral relatives by extending the terms brother and sister to cover uncles and aunts, while father and mother were applied to grandparents and great-grandparents. These arrangements accord with a social system that was strongly focused on the individual rather than on any kinship group.

Of necessity, entire peasant families engaged in farm work at peak seasons, such as planting and harvest times. Among the Inkas, farming was an activity involving both men and women. Inka men turned the soil with their *taqllas,* or foot plows, while their wives stuck tubers and seeds into the ground. The Yorubas, Aztecs, Mesopotamians, and Egyptians viewed farm labor primarily as men's work. In all the early civilizations women cooked, cleaned the houses, and looked after the children. They also spun thread and wove most of the cloth needed by their families—both time-consuming tasks. In large extended families, such as those of the Yorubas, women were able to share household labor more than in small nuclear families, such as those of the ancient Egyptians. In particular, the care of children could be left to grandmothers and older daughters, making it easier for mothers to pursue activities outside the home. Many Yoruba and Aztec women worked as traders, selling farm produce, cooked food, and manufactured goods at local markets. Yoruba women also participated in intercity trade. These activities permitted some women to acquire considerable wealth and to become financially independent of their husbands. Even among the strongly patrilineal Yorubas, women had the right to pass the wealth they had acquired through their own efforts on to their children.

In all the early civilizations, women as well as men served as priests, although the most important positions were generally reserved for men. Most officials and bureaucrats were male. Inka, Maya, and Egyptian queens exercised a subordinate role alongside their husbands not only in rituals but also in administrative activities. In Mesopotamia, kings' wives managed large estates and their daughters were made high priestesses in an effort to consolidate royal control over cities. In Shang China some women, probably wives of the king, played important roles in the palace bureaucracy, served as royal envoys, and in at least one instance commanded armies. These women seem to have performed many of the same tasks that palace eunuchs were to do in China in later times. Since these women probably came from various noble families and different parts of the kingdom, they brought with them knowledge that allowed them to carry out important administrative duties. In Aztec and other highland Mexican societies, on the other hand, the female members of royal families appear to have had little, if any, public role.

There is no obvious correlation between the varied kinship systems and types of family organization and either the environmental settings or political structures of these civilizations. It seems as if a considerable variety of domestic arrangements was compatible with the hierarchical structures and administration that were necessary to maintain these societies. Because of this, it is likely that the relations between men and women and the organization of family life that prevailed in each region before the rise of civilization played a significant role in determining specific aspects of the kinship organizations that were associated with each civilization.

Changes in some other aspects of family life appear to have been more unilinear. Women were subordinate to men in all of the early civilizations, both in public and with respect to decision-making inside the family. Relations between the sexes were colored by pervasive inequality and therefore were probably more unequal that in many, but not all, earlier societies. There is historical evidence that the freedom of women declined as a result of the rise of both the Aztec and the Inka states (Brumfiel 1991; Silverblatt 1987). Yet the role of women in the early civilizations does not seem to have been generally as disadvantaged as it was to become in many later preindustrial societies, such as those of classical Greece and Rome.

The social and legal position of women also appears to have been more favorable among the Yorubas, Inkas, Mayas, and possibly the Chinese than it was among the Aztecs and Mesopotamians. Ancient

Egyptian society was exceptional in the degree to which women enjoyed equality before the law; even when married they had the right to manage their own property and to sell or bequeath it to whomever they wished. Egyptian men, on the other hand, seem to have been obliged to leave at least one-third of their possessions to their widows.

In general, the position of women appears to have been more favorable in territorial states than it was in city-state systems, perhaps because life at the peasant level in territorial states was less transformed from what it had been prior to the rise of the state and because upper class women had more political roles to play in the small ruling elites of these societies. Yet the relatively high position of women in Yoruba society warns us that these arguments should not be pushed too far. It seems that specific cultural traditions exerted an important influence, alongside structural considerations, in shaping the role played by men and women in early civilizations.

Land Ownership

Because agriculture played such an important role in the economy of the early civilizations, patterns of land ownership might be expected to be crucial for understanding these societies. Yet we find an unexpected amount of variation in forms of landholding.

It has been argued that in many, if not all, early civilizations kings or gods claimed eminent domain over the whole land. Many early commentators suggested that this concept excluded the possibility of private ownership; everyone being in effect a tenant, if not a slave, of the king. In general, however, such claims as were made by early rulers seem to have amounted to no more than an assertion of sovereignty, equivalent to those made by modern states. Among the Yorubas, for example, land could not be sold or given to foreigners without obtaining the permission of the king. The king, however, did not have the right to possess any land that belonged to his people.

In some of the early civilizations, large amounts of land were owned collectively. The Aztec *calpulli* was above all an endogamous landowning group. Each calpulli had its own headman, selected from a specific lineage, as well as its own deity, cult center, and school. Its able-bodied men constituted a separate regiment in the Aztec army. The population of the Aztec capital was divided among twenty (some say eighty) calpullis. Most calpulli members were full-time or part-time farmers but urban calpullis also contained substantial numbers of full-time artisans, such as goldworkers, lapidaries, potters, and feather workers; a single craft was usually associated with a specific calpulli. The calpullis made up of long-distance traders and the royal family probably contained no farmers, although the members of these groups owned land that was worked for them by others. While in some parts of Mexico calpulli land was regularly reassigned to accord with the changing needs of member families, this does not appear to have been the practice in the southern part of the Basin of Mexico. As a result, individual families within the core of the Aztec empire came to hold unequal amounts of land. If the occupant did not wish to work some or all of his land, he could rent it to someone else. No one, however, had the right to sell or expropriate calpulli territory. If a particular family died out, its share of land automatically reverted to the collectivity.

Highland Peruvian society was similarly made up of a large number of *ayllus*. Each ayllu collectively possessed its own land, and had its own hereditary leader and cults. Every family was allotted a share of land sufficient for its needs, which were reapportioned on a regular basis. The members of an ayllu assisted each other to cultivate their land and carry out collective labor projects that benefited the entire group. They were also responsible for attending to the needs of members of the group who were sick, orphaned, or called away to work on state labor projects.

Among the Yorubas, the most important landholding group was the patrilineal extended family; only unclaimed land belonged to the community. Each extended family would own the plot of land on which its compound stood in an urban center, as well as plots of farmland at various distances from the town. This farmland was inalienable and some of it was worked for the support of family chiefs and corporate activities. The rest was divided among the individual families that made up the extended family. The total amount of land that was owned varied according to the wealth and status of particular extended families. These factors also determined whether the land was worked primarily by family members, dependents, or slaves.

In Shang China, the situation is less clear. Blocks of land appear to have been worked by patrilineal extended families (*tsu*), but we are uncertain whether these groups owned the land. The fact that government decrees relocated extended families from one part of the kingdom to another and assigned them to serve new lords suggests that at least some extended families worked, but did not own, the land. Tsus persisted over approximately seven genera-tions and the largest of them contained about a hundred nuclear families. At this stage fissioning occurred as some groups moved away to occupy new land.

In Mesopotamia, extended families owned large tracts of land, but even in the earliest documented periods such land could be sold subject to the collective agreement of its owners. In the course of the third millennium B.C., holdings of this sort appear to have been converted into privately or institutionally owned land at an acceler-ating rate. As a result, land of this sort must have accounted for an ever-declining portion of the total.

For Old Kingdom Egypt, the situation is far from clear. During this period, ever more estates were created for the benefit of the crown, royal cult establishments, and temples. We do not know, however, whether prior to that time each village had owned its own land and to what extent this form of ownership might have persisted in areas unaffected by the creation of estates. It is also unclear if the creation of estates extinguished existing peasant communities' rights to the soil, or if these communities were incorporated into estates with their land rights intact but subject to additional obligations to pay rents to the estate. While it has been asserted that little land re-mained under the corporate control of villages, one small settle-ment, Nag⁏ al-Deir, displayed remarkable social continuity through the Old Kingdom—although it became less egalitarian and gener-ally more impoverished as the economic demands of the state increased during the Third and Fourth Dynasties (Reisner 1932). For ancient Egypt, it is impossible to determine much about the nature of social and economic relations that fell outside or below the purview of official interest and hence written records.

In every early civilization, there were also privileged forms of landholding. Each Aztec calpulli set aside land that was worked by all its members for the support of the calpulli's leader and temple.

Within each city state in the Mexican highlands, local rulers inherited land as part of their royal patrimonial possessions, while other land was reserved for the support of government officials and important state activities, such as waging war. Plots of land were exchanged as marriage presents among the rulers of different city states. Aztec kings also granted land in conquered territories to victorious warriors, members of the nobility, and to Aztec temples at the state and calpulli levels. This land was worked by local farmers under the supervision of Aztec state officials and the surplus produce delivered to its owners. As a result of these transactions, rulers, nobles, and outstanding warriors often owned or had the use of land in several different city states. This helped to cement alliances among allied states and stiffened the resolve of members of hegemonic states to ensure that their city remained dominant. Much of this land was cultivated not by *macehualli*, or 'free commoners,' but by *mayeque*, or 'serfs.' These individuals were bound to the soil and did not pay taxes, but were required to serve in the army and remained subject to the laws of their city state. While the calpullis retained possession of their communal lands in the Aztec city state and among the Aztecs' closest allies, it appears that an increasing amount of land in adjacent parts of the Aztec Empire was rapidly falling under the control of the Aztec state and individual high-ranking Aztecs.

Prior to the Inka conquest, each ayllu, like each Mexican calpulli, had apparently set aside land for the support of its leader and his family and for the group's ritual activities. Following their conquest, the Inkas expropriated additional land to support the state and the religious cults it established and patronized throughout the empire. To prevent undue hardship to peasants, at least part of this land appears to have been physically brought into existence after the Inka conquest through extra terracing and hydraulic works rather than created by confiscating existing holdings. Peasants were obliged to cultivate this land before working their own, but were provided with seed by the government institutions and temples to whom the land belonged. The peasants also had to be fed by these institutions as long as they worked such land. In return, the entire harvest belonged to the state or temple. Ayllu members were also conscripted to tend herds belonging to the state and to temples.

The Inka king attempted to increase state revenues by creating large estates which he assigned to himself, to the cults of dead rulers, to members of the nobility, and to the support of the army. These lands were tax-free and, after being assigned to individuals, were inherited by all of their descendants. Like ayllu lands, they could not be sold, transferred, or divided. The peasants who had originally owned these lands often were resettled in other parts of the empire. Estates were cultivated either by corvée labor, which was brought from elsewhere to work for short periods of time, or by *yanacona*, peasants who had been removed from their communities and turned into serfs. The percentage of the harvest that the government and members of the upper classes collected from these estates greatly exceeded what they could have obtained as taxes from land worked by ayllus. There is evidence that the amount of land held in this fashion was increasing rapidly in the final years of Inka rule.

In Mesopotamia, far more land was institutionally or privately owned when the earliest written records become available than was the case among the Aztecs and Inkas. The main owners were temples, palaces, and a small number of princely families. Some kin-based communities persisted inside and outside these estates, but such groups appear to have been gradually losing their control of land as a result of collective sales. The estates were partly cultivated by laborers, who were paid with subsistence rations and by being assigned small parcels of land which they cultivated to supply the rest of their needs. Other portions of these estates were share-cropped or rented to small farmers. State and temple officials were frequently paid for their services by being assigned the use of moderate sized tracts of land. These could in turn be rented, share-cropped, or worked with paid laborers to produce an income. All of the land on temple estates, by whatever contractual arrangement it was cultivated, appears to have been supplied with seed, draft animals, plowmen, and equipment from central stores. The peak demand for agricultural labor was partly supplied by gangs of day laborers who followed the planting and harvest from south to north through Mesopotamia each fall and spring. Aside from slaves, these must have been among the poorest members of society.

In Old Kingdom Egypt, estates existed by the reign of Snefru (ca. 2600 B.C.). The most important of these were owned directly by the crown and some were used to support the king and his relatives. Others were created to provide for the funerary cults of kings and high-ranking officials, this task being assumed as a royal responsibility. Still other estates belonged to temples and private individuals. Revenues from these estates circulated in highly complex ways. A private tomb might receive food supplies from royal property and cult lands, special land endowments, and private funerary estates, as well as through the contractual reversion, or re-use, of offerings from royal funerary cults, temples, and other tombs. This income supported the low-ranking officials who attended to the tomb's ongoing funerary cult.

Officials and royal kin were able to derive wealth from privately owned lands that they inherited, purchased, or were given by the state, from lands that they held so long as they performed official duties, and from payments that they received for performing priestly offices in temples and royal mortuary cults. By appointing government officials to priestly offices relating to funerary cults, it was possible for kings to return to administrative use some of the increasing amounts of land that were being devoted to such cults. The government also appears to have been actively developing new estates, especially in the underpopulated Delta region. These were peopled with peasants from elsewhere in Egypt and prisoners of war, who were destined to become peasants. It is not clear, however, to what extent peasants were free to move—or could be forced to move—from one region to another. Their apparent scarcity suggests that it might not have been easy to prevent adventurous peasants from moving to areas of economic development, where working conditions were probably more favorable.

Estates assigned to support specific government institutions or the funerary cults of high-ranking individuals were widely distributed throughout Egypt. This gave government officials a vested interest in supporting the unity of the state. It is very difficult for any time in Egyptian history to determine how much land was owned freehold by individuals or as some kind of conditional, though often inheritable, grant from the crown. Even records of land sales do not always resolve this question, since it is often not clear whether freeholds or use-rights were being transferred.

It is tempting to see varying combinations of collective, institutional, and private ownership of land constituting an evolutionary sequence that can be used to separate early civilizations into more and less advanced types. To some extent this interpretation appears to be borne out by developmental changes observed within the Aztec, Inka, Mesopotamian, and Egyptian civilizations, although only in the latter two are these sequences of long duration. Yet the equally well attested long-term viability of many different forms of land ownership indicates that all these forms were compatible with early civilizations as a general stage of development. Here too we seem to be dealing with an aspect of social organization in which historical particularities played a significant role.

Taxation

The principal economic feature common to all the early civilizations was the institutionalized appropriation of surpluses from the lower classes by the ruling group. Because the early civilizations were based on agriculture, most of the appropriation took place in terms of foodstuffs, which peasants were induced to produce and then surrender to the upper classes. Aztec calpulli members, in addition to supporting their corporate institutions, paid a grain tax to the central government. In Peru and possibly in China, as well as to some extent in highland Mexico, the grain tax took the form of cultivating fields belonging to the state or to members of the nobility. In Old Kingdom Egypt, taxes were levied on grain and livestock produced by estates and peasant communities. These taxes were fixed by a biennial census, which in early times probably involved the king and his court traveling up and down the country and consuming part of what was due on the spot. Later, tax revenues were amassed in kind in the provincial (*sp3t*) capitals, from which revenues not required to manage government affairs at the local level were forwarded to the royal court at Memphis.

At the same time, surplus agricultural production flowed into the hands of the upper classes in the form of rents, which were paid by peasants to landowners and landholders. In the case of the Aztecs, these included the fees paid by farmers for land they rented from calpulli members who did not engage in agriculture themselves and the produce owed to members of the nobility by the serfs who worked their estates. Another arrangement, which was generally even more favorable to the landholder, was sharecropping. This short-term contract with a tenant farmer required the landholder to invest more of his own capital in the production of a crop and to assume more risk, but gave him a significantly larger share of the crop. Among the Yorubas, the direct taxation of agricultural production took the form of presenting only token amounts of food to the king or his representatives at annual festivals. However, the Yoruba king and members of the nobility derived revenues from taxing food being brought into the cities for everyday consumption, presumably even from the farms where it was grown. The Yoruba upper classes also owned large estates, which were worked for them mainly by slaves and debtors.

Governments derived further revenues by taxing the sale and movement of a wide variety of goods. The Yorubas levied tolls on raw materials and manufactured goods passing between states and through city gates. The Aztec state taxed market sales and the ancient Egyptians are reported to have had to surrender a portion of their handicraft production to the government. In all of the early civilizations, corvée labor was extracted from commoners, especially during slack periods in the agricultural cycle. Among the Aztecs this involved military service, working on state construction projects, serving in royal palaces, and keeping public areas of the city clean. The Inka rulers fed, clothed, and housed those who performed corvée labor and this seems to have been done in Egypt as well. Aztec armies were supplied with food by conquered states located along their march routes. In most early civilizations, peasant women were required to weave cloth for landowners and the state; Hekanakhte expected his tenants' wives to produce cloth for him.

All of these arrangements resulted in a disproportionately large amount of the surplus production and labor of the lower classes falling under the control of a small ruling elite. Because of this, it mattered less who owned land than who had the right to control agricultural surpluses and peasant labor. This explains why a wide variety of landowning and landholding systems and many different ways of taxing goods were able to support very similar sociopolitical structures. It also justifies the suggestion that these societies shared a common tributary mode of production (Amin 1976:9–16). The basic features of this mode of production were the ability of a privileged elite to extract substantial surpluses from commoners and that, contrary to arrangements in modern societies, the control of these surpluses was more important than the ownership of property. The level of agricultural productivity in the early civilizations was so low that in territorial states it probably required at least nine peasant families to support a single family that did not produce food. Since the latter included those of full-time craftsmen as well as of bureaucrats and members of the nobility, the number of families whose members were exempt from all forms of manual labor was considerably fewer. Because of the somewhat more efficient productive systems in city states, it is possible that the ratio of non-food producers to peasants there was somewhat higher.

Authority

Rulers and officials in all of the early civilizations sought to project an image of power and authority. In ancient Egypt the stick and whip were symbols of office and a few scenes in Old Kingdom tombs depict local scribes being flogged in the presence of high-ranking officials for failing to deliver the required taxes. Yet, in reality, there were serious limits to the exercise of power in the early civilizations. In societies where productive capacities were severely limited, a ruling class would not be inclined to utilize resources for managerial purposes that reached far beyond the minimum that was necessary to perpetuate the system, since doing so increased administrative costs, thus diminishing the resources that the ruling class could use for its own purposes. One way to minimize administrative costs was to delegate power from higher to lower levels in an administrative hierarchy, a practice that in the past led scholars to see evidence of feudal structures in the early civilizations.

While numerous titles existed which suggest a detailed division of labor in the administration of most early civilizations, powers were often not specifically defined and higher-level offices tended to confer a general and far-reaching, rather than a clearly defined, authority on their holders. The Egyptian viziers (_t3ty_) carried out many functions at the national or (if there was more than one vizier) the regional level and provincial governors did the same in their districts. This wholesale delegation of power was a relatively inexpensive and structurally undemanding way to administer a large preindustrial state. That bureaucracies were relatively undifferentiated suggests that rulers were rarely willing, or able, to assume the economic and administrative burdens necessary to control the lower levels of their administrations more effectively.

There is also evidence that much self-regulation was tolerated, and even encouraged, at lower levels. Aztec calpullis, Peruvian ayllus, and Egyptian communities through their *kenbets*, which were both councils and judicial courts, were left to regulate their internal affairs; state intervention occurred only when this regulation had clearly failed to work. The same was true of the Yoruba extended family, which constituted a political and religious as well as a landowning unit under the presidency of its oldest male member. The *bale*, or head of a Yoruba compound, usually its oldest male, could order its members to be fined, chained, flogged, or imprisoned. The most common limitation on the power of such groups was the requirement that death sentences they imposed on their members had to be referred to higher officials, and perhaps ultimately to the king, for approval. By allowing local groups to manage their own affairs, the higher levels of government spared themselves numerous difficulties and administrative costs.

Exemplary, often cruel, punishments were inflicted on criminals—especially traitors and those who had committed offenses against the state, temples, and members of the nobility. Yet such punishments were often an indication of the weakness rather than the strength of law enforcement. Archaeological settlement patterns suggest that the maintenance of law and order was not as effective as the rulers of the early civilizations would have liked it to be. In all of the early civilizations, temples, palaces, and state storage facilities were surrounded by strong enclosure walls that, in addition to marking the sanctity and importance of such institutions, protected them against intruders. Likewise, houses, especially those of wealthy families, tended to open onto inner courtyards. Such houses often had only a single guarded entrance from the street and no external windows, at least not on the ground floor. That the Aztecs, Inkas, Yorubas, Mesopotamians, Egyptians (at sites such as the Middle Kingdom one at Kahun), and probably the Shang Chinese all created houses of this sort—and that such houses were common in urban centers—indicate a concern for security at the family level and a distrust of the effectiveness of state authority.

Large New Kingdom Egyptian houses such as those excavated at Amarna, which were built inside walled enclosures, and Maya house complexes, which faced onto central courtyards, provide further examples of a concern for security at the family level.

The legal systems that were administered by the central governments suggest that these governments wished to minimize their direct involvement in maintaining order. Law codes, such as that of the Mesopotamian king Hammurabi, claimed to embody the monarch's desire to dispense justice in such a manner as to protect the weak from the powerful. Yet in this code and many others commoners were punished more severely for offenses committed against the upper classes than upper class people were for crimes they committed against commoners. The one exception was the Aztec legal system, which punished nobles more severely for a wide range of offenses, including drunkenness, than it did commoners. Nobles were assumed to be endowed with stronger spiritual powers than were commoners and hence able to resist temptation more resolutely. This made their misbehavior a betrayal of class ideals.

Furthermore, in all these societies, commoners who contemplated seeking legal redress against nobles knew that they would have to face judges who belonged to the upper classes and whose natural sympathies would be with members of their own class. Members of the upper class also had more resources to bribe judges. In addition, severe penalties were often inflicted on those who brought unprovable charges against someone. The unlikelihood of winning a case must have deterred all but the most determined commoners from pressing charges against their superiors. Contrariwise, the threat of legal action permitted nobles to coerce members of the lower classes (Offner 1983:82). Hence the legal system tended to reinforce the power of the upper classes, while discouraging ordinary people from having recourse to it. The Egyptian "Tale of the Eloquent Peasant," which describes how the king rescued someone wrongly accused of theft by a powerful official, is overtly a story about justice being done to a common man. Yet it carried the message that justice was really done in that case only because the peasant's exceptional eloquence had entertained the king (Lichtheim 1973:169–84). All of this suggests that in early civilizations the state was not anxious to expend energy by intervening in aspects of human behavior that could be kept self-regulating.

The Army

Additional evidence for such a policy is the limited force that officials actually had at their disposal. Wars against other states were normally waged by armies composed of conscripted commoners led by nobles, only a few of whom were full-time military officers. Every Aztec boy was trained to be a soldier, most of them in the *telpochcalli* or 'boys' schools' run by the calpullis. Yoruba armies were raised by the leaders of patrilineages amongst their kinsmen, followers, and slaves. The Inka, Egyptian, and Chinese states also raised conscript armies. In some instances territorial states were able to use conscripts from one part of their large kingdoms to suppress uprisings in other parts. Elman Service (1975) has maintained that conscript armies were the only armed force available to the rulers of the early civilizations, and on these grounds has proposed that the early civilizations were not true states but chiefdom-like theocracies. Morton Fried (1967) disagrees, arguing that physical force played an important role in the management of early civilizations.

The Aztec state promoted commoner soldiers who had captured at least four prisoners of war to the rank of *quauhpilli*, or 'semi-nobles,' and granted them estates or revenues that exempted them from the need to perform manual labor. In return, these warriors were required to serve as guards at the royal palace for part of each year and to protect the state's supplies of weapons, which were stored between campaigns in armories near the main temples. They also trained young warriors, arrested people when ordered to do so by royal officials, and formed elite corps within the army. They and the hereditary nobles who led the Aztec army constituted a sizable body of professional soldiers at the disposal of the state.

In Mesopotamia, at least by Early Dynastic III times, kings controlled professional, well-trained military units equipped with metal helmets, specialized weapons, and uniforms. Some of these soldiers battled from chariots, but most were armed with long spears and fought on foot in phalanx formations. These soldiers probably formed the nucleus of the larger conscript armies that served the state in wartime. The increasing intercity conflicts that encouraged the creation of corps of professional soldiers also provided the justification for Mesopotamian military leaders to increase their landholdings and to dominate the political life of cities. Revenues from the royal estates paid for manufacturing military equipment and professional soldiers were granted land to support themselves and their families. Unlike Aztec professional soldiers, who remained members of their calpullis, Mesopotamian ones were bound to their kings by closer and more personal economic and social ties.

Among the Yorubas, whose city states were politically the least centralized in my sample, even Oyo, the largest kingdom, had no national standing army. Yet in wartime, lineage heads and the rulers of subordinate towns were obliged to supply soldiers and food for the army. They were also responsible for training their followers and helping to arm them. In addition to recruiting troops from among his followers, each chief supported a number of full-time soldiers who acted as his bodyguard. Some of these were equipped with horses. Ambitious chiefs sought to acquire large numbers of male slaves to perform agricultural work and to augment the numbers of recruits available for military campaigns. The Oyo army was not led by the king, as it was at least in theory in most other early civilizations, but by the Basorun, a high official who headed a different patrilineal group from that of the monarch. Despite its decentralized nature, the Oyo army was for several centuries a powerful force in West Africa. The kings of Benin, who were politically more powerful than those of the Yorubas, recruited a large number of young men who acted as their bodyguard, messengers, and to enforce their will. For as long as they served the king, these men were forbidden to marry or wear clothes. Yoruba kings had a much smaller number of male retainers, who, among other duties, served as their bodyguard.

Apart from a significant difference in scale, the military arrangements in territorial states were generally similar to those in city states. From an early period, the Chinese rulers did not depend only on conscripts levied by subordinate rulers but also established a standing army that in the Western Chou period was composed of fourteen divisions, eight of which were stationed around the royal administrative center of Ch'êng-chou. They also garrisoned many frontier forts. The problems posed by the dual need to defend the exposed borders of the Chinese state and to curb internal divisiveness probably explain the existence of a large professional army.

The Inkas likewise, in addition to utilizing peasant levies, were engaged in creating a professional army. Those drawn into these forces were men from specific ethnic groups noted for their valor and individual peasants who had displayed notable courage and resourcefulness in battle. These soldiers and their families were excused from paying any form of tax other than their military service. Unlike the military conscripts, who remained in the army for only a short period, professional soldiers appear to have served throughout their active life. Control over regiments of seasoned veterans (who had served under his father in the prolonged wars which that king had waged on the northern frontiers of the empire), assured Atawallpa, the last Inka king, victory over the larger forces of his half-brother Waskhar in their struggle for succession to the throne. The creation of such regiments eliminated the need to rotate conscripts in the middle of long campaigns, increased the level of professionalism within the army, and created forces loyal to the king rather than to local lords. In Cuzco, the king had a palace guard composed of two thousand soldiers, as well as a personal bodyguard of one hundred high-ranking officers. Garrisons and border forts were defended by settlers chosen for their loyalty to the Inka state. The families assigned this duty rotated their tasks: everyone helped to grow food for the group, while the men took turns guarding the fort.

We are relatively poorly informed about the armies of Old and Middle Kingdom Egypt. Foreign wars seem to have been fought largely with peasant conscripts, but the royal court, provincial administrative centers, and border fortifications must have been guarded by professional soldiers. Companies of Egyptian spearmen and Nubian archers are depicted marching in formation in models from the tomb of Mesehti at Asyut (Trigger 1976:202). Mercenaries, recruited from among the Medjay, a pastoral people who lived in the Eastern Desert, appear to have served as a police force. One of their tasks was to help collect taxes from recalcitrant peasants. For operations of this sort Egyptian officials may have preferred to rely on foreigners. The Egyptian army became larger and more professionalized after the start of the New Kingdom, when chariots and other new weapons were introduced. In Ramesside times, increasing numbers of foreign mercenaries were drawn into a standing army. Individual soldiers were remunerated by being granted farms or small estates.

Yet, despite the evidence for professional soldiers in all of the early civilizations, Service is correct that armed force does not appear to have been as important, or the military institutionally as autonomous, as they were to be in many later and more complex preindustrial civilizations. Moreover, while some professional soldiers were wholly freed from manual labor, others appear to have spent part of their time cultivating their land grants. They differed from peasant conscripts mainly in the extent of their military training, their equipment, and their obligations for military service. This may partially explain the relative ease and speed with which the Aztec, Inka, and Yoruba states succumbed when challenged by more highly organized European military forces. It also raises an interesting question concerning the level of exploitation in early civilizations.

Inequality

It is difficult to measure degrees of exploitation in the early civilizations. Long ago Ulrich Wilcken estimated that the Ptolemaic government extracted about ten times more wealth from the Egyptian people than had been collected previously (Weber 1976:226). While both the population and the productivity of Egypt were significantly greater in the Ptolemaic period than they had been before, this still indicates a higher level of exploitation than in earlier times. Likewise, slavery appears to have been a less extensive and less oppressive institution in the early civilizations than it was in classical Greek and Roman society. Herodotus reported that Khufu and Khafre, the builders of the two biggest pyramids at Giza, were remembered as tyrants who had ignored the worship of the gods and oppressed the people, while their successor, Menkaure, who had built the much smaller third pyramid, was celebrated as a generous and good king. Herodotus' account has been dismissed as a dragoman's invention or alternatively been interpreted as a garbled memory of Akhenaton's reign (Aldred 1968:260). Yet it rings true to the archaeological evidence and to the way ancient civilizations worked. If the first two kings had pushed their personal demands on the economy to the point where their behavior endangered the unity of the state, Menkaure made a timely adjustment, after which no ruler (except perhaps Akhenaton) ever tried to monopolize the wealth of Egypt for his own ends to such an extent again. All of this evidence suggests that exploitation was not as severe in the early civilizations as it was in many more developed preindustrial ones.

Authority did not go unchallenged in any early civilization. We know that the failure of the state to pay royal tomb builders soon led to rowdy demonstrations in the late New Kingdom (Bierbrier 1982:41). Moreover, despite their divine or divinely protected status, many kings in the early civilizations who proved to be weak, or excessively tyrannical, fell victim to assassination, and Egyptian kings were no exception. Yet no one in the early civilizations appears to have challenged the concept of a system based upon inequality or its claim to reflect the natural order established by the gods at the time of creation.

The early civilizations were societies in which inequality was accepted as a normal condition and injustice viewed as a personal rather than a systemic evil (Weber 1976:258). Every child was born into a family that had been shaped in the image of the state. The subordination of child to parent, and to varying degrees of wife to husband, went fundamentally unquestioned, as did corporal punishment as a means of enforcing obedience and discipline (Trigger 1985b). It was a world in which the terms 'father,' 'king,' and 'god' were metaphors for each other and for power. If peasant communities had been egalitarian prior to the rise of the state (which was not always the case), none remained so afterwards. These communities had their own gradations of power and wealth; their most advantaged members strengthened their positions by acting as intermediaries between their fellow villagers and the state. This refutes Karl Marx's model of the Asiatic mode of production, which assumed that in the early civilizations egalitarian peasant communities constituted the unchanging economic basis of exploitative states (Marx 1964; Bailey and Llobera 1981). Because of the pervasiveness of inequality, no one who lived in the early civilizations questioned the normalcy of this condition. If egalitarianism was known, it was as a feature of some of the despised, barbarian societies that existed beyond the borders of the 'civilized' world.

Peasants were also locked into a situation in which their well-being depended on rulers who could defend them from external attack and maintain the internal order on which the systems of production had come to depend. Because they made their lives possible, the benefits that rulers provided to peasants were far from intangible. Hence, so long as rulers did not exploit their subjects beyond conventional limits, their rule was accepted. Capable rulers recognized this and took care not to alienate the passive support of the peasantry by overtaxing or otherwise oppressing them (Weber 1976:63). They also encouraged support by rewarding their more active followers with gifts and offering them opportunities for personal betterment. While the presents that rulers gave to higher officials often were of substantial value, peasants normally received from government officials and priests only a special allotment of beer and meat on feast days, a small return of what the peasants themselves had paid in taxes. Yet so long as a show of goodwill was maintained, the benefits of a system that worked outweighed the evident lack of reciprocity in material goods. The next chapter will examine the political means by which order and equilibrium were maintained in the early civilizations.

Three

Politics and Culture

Political and economic power in the early civilizations were closely linked and reinforced rather than competed with one another. It has recently been argued that sociopolitical forces were more important determinants of preindustrial, class-divided societies than were economic forces (Giddens 1981), and that even the modern world system is shaped by political factors no less than by economic ones (Giddens 1985). It is clear that in the early civilizations political power was a necessary means to obtain and protect wealth, while the control of wealth was essential to maintain power. But unlike in a modern industrial society, there appears to have been little opportunity for economic and political interests to compete with one another (Eisenstadt 1963). This is strikingly demonstrated by the total exclusion from political life of merchants whose wealth was derived solely from commercial gain. Whether an analyst assigns causal primacy to sociopolitical or economic factors, or rejects this distinction as a false dichotomy (Edens 1992:134), any functional analysis of early civilizations requires that economic and sociopolitical factors be treated as parallel and mutually reinforcing.

Class Hierarchy

Every early civilization had a class and status hierarchy which, like the tributary method of appropriating surpluses described in the last chapter, was generally similar, although differing in detail, from one early civilization to another. In these societies, social mobility was carefully controlled from the top, even though the need to learn most skills from parents or close relatives greatly restricted it in any case.

At the top of each hierarchy stood a king, whose principal duty was to see that the system worked. Kings were responsible for the defense of the realm, for maintaining order, and for managing relations with the supernatural. Kingship generally descended patrilineally, either from father to son or among brothers, before passing to the next generation. In some states not included in our sample, such as that of the Ashantes of modern Ghana, it was inherited matrilineally. In these cases, however, kings sought to marry in such a way as to ensure that their descendants inherited the throne (Wilks 1975:371). Because of the need for effective military leadership, only in rare and exceptional circumstances did women wield royal power and then usually only as regents. For the same reason, the inheritance of kingship was rarely determined by male primogeniture. Among the Inkas and the ancient Egyptians, the throne ideally passed to a son of the king by his principal wife—yet the king appears to have had the right to decide which of his sons was best suited to succeed him. In Egypt, to conduct the funeral of the previous ruler was a further requirement for succession. In both societies, the death of a king was regarded as a time of crisis and armed conflicts to decide the succession were not unknown. In an effort to avoid such conflicts, heirs were sometimes publicly designated, or even installed as co-rulers, during their predecessor's reign.

The Aztec king was chosen from among the male members of the royal patrilineage by a council composed of the highest officers of the realm, most of whom were members of the royal family. In making this selection, the military and political skills of each candidate were carefully scrutinized. Another branch of the Aztec royal family monopolized a second office, that of the *cihuacoatl*, which means literally 'Snake Woman.' This official, who despite his title was a man, acted as regent when the king died or was absent from the city, supervised many routine fiscal and legal matters, and was regarded by the Aztecs as a co-ruler, though subordinate politically to the king, or *tlatoani*. This Aztec dual kingship was modeled on their concept of the supreme divinity, the 'Lord and Lady of Duality,' with the Snake Woman representing the female side. In less tightly integrated realms, such as those of the Yorubas and possibly the early Shang Chinese, the kingship rotated among a number of patrilineages belonging to the royal clan. In some still less powerful highland Mexican and Yoruba states, several 'kings,' heading different ethnic or kinship groups, ruled these groups simultaneously, while cooperating to govern the realm.

The king was also the leader of the nobility. This class was hierarchically ordered: the highest rank usually consisted of the immediate members of the royal family, followed by descendants of previous kings, members of other powerful families—including ones whose ancestors had ruled states that had been incorporated into the realm—and finally descendants of individuals who had been promoted to noble rank in recognition of their abilities and service to the state. While the composition of the nobility and the formality of its definition tended to vary from one civilization to another, membership in this class, once achieved, was usually hereditary. Nobles were exempt from physical labor and enjoyed a comfortable lifestyle that was supported by family and personal landholdings, government subsidies, and the emoluments they received for the state offices they held. While not all noblemen held public office, the highest administrative, religious, and military positions in the state were filled by members of this class. The nobility thus played a major role in decision-making and administration and its leading members to varying degrees shared power with the king. Among the Yorubas, for example, responsibilities for various governmental tasks were divided among the leaders of high-ranking lineage groups. Wealth and power depended upon retaining control of particular offices and continuing to forge marriage alliances with royalty and other leading families. A noble lineage that failed to do this was destined to decline in power and wealth over time.

Next in the hierarchy was a mixed group that is often labeled a 'middle class,' although this term is a misnomer since the political and economic status of these people differed radically from that of the bourgeoisie in modern societies. I propose to call them 'dependent specialists.' Some members of this group may have owned small estates and hence enjoyed a certain degree of financial independence. Most of them, however, depended upon the state or upon members of the nobility for much of their income, which took the form of salaries, rights to use land, and direct payments for services. The members of this class lacked political power and were in effect clients of the state or of individual members of the nobility for whom they worked.

Within this group there was a marked social stratification, depending on whether the work an individual did more closely resembled that done by nobles or peasants. The highest-ranking members of this class were minor bureaucrats, who kept records and carried out administrative tasks but did not set policies. They included scribes, full-time priests, and high-ranking artists and engineers. These individuals, together with the more educated members of the nobility, monopolized the specialized technical knowledge that was available in early civilizations. Like the nobility, they did not labor with their hands. The Middle Kingdom "Satire on the Professions" genre reflects the scorn with which ancient Egyptian scribes regarded those who were socially inferior to them (Lichtheim 1973:184–92).

Also of *de facto* high status in some of the early civilizations were merchants who engaged in long-distance trade. They supplied the luxury goods desired by the nobility and successful merchants became quite wealthy. Yet, for reasons we shall consider below, they were unable to transform their wealth into political power and even their social standing was often fraught with ambiguity.

Next in the hierarchy of dependent specialists came professional soldiers. They worked with their hands rather than with their heads, but like the higher orders they did not produce anything tangible. Their commanders were usually members of the nobility. Of markedly lower status were the full-time craftsmen, the most important of whom were the specialists who produced luxury goods for the upper classes. Some of these craftsmen sold their products to the upper classes; others were employed by the state or by members of the nobility. Despite their skills, craftsmen were regarded as inferior to the dependent specialists we have already considered because, like peasants, they worked with their hands. Nevertheless, because their products were highly valued, they lived far more comfortably than did most peasants.

A final group of dependent specialists were the attendants who looked after the personal needs of the king and members of the nobility. Most were manual laborers, and they constituted the lowest level of dependent specialists. However, those individuals who attended directly on major figures might derive considerable personal influence from their position. In ancient Egypt, Peru, and highland Mexico, dwarfs and hunchbacks, who were not considered suited for agricultural labor, were recruited as attendants for the king and the nobility. In Old Kingdom Egypt, some of them were either trained as goldsmiths or placed in charge of goldwork. It has been suggested that this was because they were easily recognizable and hence could be apprehended easily if they attempted to steal anything. This does not, however, account for the more general use of dwarfs as personal servants by the nobility. Some attendants who won royal favor were made members of the nobility.

The peasant class was by far the most populous in the early civilizations and must have constituted at least 80 percent of the total population. As we have seen in Chapter Two, while peasants were regarded as free members of society, their legal status varied considerably both within and among the ancient civilizations. In Inka and Aztec society, most peasants collectively owned the land they worked; while the rest were bound as serfs to land owned by the state or the nobility. Both groups enjoyed security of tenure but did not have the freedom to move elsewhere. In Egypt and Mesopotamia, some peasants may have owned freeholds, but their tenure was easily lost as a consequence of indebtedness. As institutional and private ownership of land increased, a growing number of peasants found themselves renting or sharecropping land, or reduced to being agricultural laborers. Each of these relations exposed them to an increasing degree of economic exploitation.

There were few slaves in the early civilizations. Many were foreigners captured in war or obtained through the slave trade. Others were citizens enslaved as a result of indebtedness (including failure to pay taxes) or as a punishment for committing crimes. The Aztecs did not acquire many slaves as a result of military action, since they sacrificed most of their prisoners to the gods. The Shang Chinese also killed large numbers of prisoners of war in religious rituals. In the Early Dynastic Period, the Mesopotamians slaughtered many male captives after battles and may have blinded others for use as unskilled laborers, but female prisoners were set to work in large weaving establishments. Presumably the Aztecs and Mesopotamians feared that it would be difficult to control large numbers of male prisoners who came from nearby states and could escape easily. The Egyptians, on the other hand, appear to have readily utilized male prisoners as agricultural laborers and mercenaries.

Not being free, slaves constituted the lowest class in society. Yet they were employed at varying levels in the early civilizations. While most worked as household servants or agricultural laborers, some became soldiers or even bureaucrats. The *ajele*, or 'agents,' whom the Alafin, or king of the hegemonic Yoruba state of Oyo, installed to keep an eye on the rulers and councils of tributary states were usually selected from among his slaves. By being inducted into the royal Shango cult, they were able, when necessary, to enter trances that made them temporarily, as embodiments of the god Shango, at least the equals of local rulers. Highly-placed slaves often were valued for not having any family interests that they might put ahead of those of their owners.

While some slaves were badly treated, especially those employed in workshops and as farm laborers, the legal condition of slaves was not as bad as it was to be in many later civilizations. Among the Aztecs, debt slaves could buy their freedom, slaves retained the right to marry and own property, and their children were born free. Some Aztec and Yoruba slaves were allowed to go on living at home, but either they or other family members had to perform a stipulated amount of work for their owners. The absorption of slaves into the general population, rather than their failure to reproduce, appears to have been the major reason their numbers remained low. In general, the upper classes depended for support on a self-sustaining peasantry rather than on slaves.

I have not reserved a special place for priests in this hierarchy. Religious activities were carried out by highly trained, full-time specialists but also on a part-time basis by volunteers or even as corvée labor. The most important positions in religious hierarchies were invariably occupied by members of the nobility, lesser ones by dependent specialists and peasants. Much of the harder physical labor associated with maintaining temples was performed by priests drawn from the peasant class. While major positions among the Aztecs were usually filled by full-time personnel and the more menial ones on a part-time basis, in Old Kingdom Egypt even high-ranking priests were government officials who performed ritual duties on a rotational basis. There is no evidence that priests constituted a special class or even a clearly demarcated order in any of the early civilizations.

Social Mobility

In the early civilizations, class mobility was extremely limited. It was most frequent in societies that were experiencing rapid internal development and in states that were acquiring hegemony over their neighbors. A buoyant economy made it possible for indigenous persons and foreigners alike to move upward in the social hierarchy. Among the Aztecs, for example, commoners who had captured at least four prisoners in battle were promoted to the lowest level of the nobility. They no longer had to perform manual labor, could live in stone houses, and were allowed to wear fine clothing and special insignia. They were also permitted to marry women from the hereditary nobility, which assured that the children of such marriages became full members of that class. On the other hand, once the Aztec empire ceased to expand, King Moctezuma II took steps to limit vertical mobility. He forbade the sons of noblemen to attend court unless they were of noble descent on their mothers' side as well (Durán 1964:222–24). This action barred sons by secondary wives and concubines from gaining access to higher offices of state, which had formerly been open to them. On the other hand, a limited number of peasants' and craftsmen's sons who demonstrated an aptitude for the priesthood or for administrative careers were allowed to attend the *calmecacs*, or 'special schools,' where the members of the nobility were instructed.

It seems likely that in Egypt and Mesopotamia a few sons of prosperous commoners were able to attend fee-charging schools and, by learning to write, rise to become scribes or even administrators. Beginning in the Old Kingdom, the literature and tomb inscriptions of Egypt stressed the ideal of the self-made and self-reliant man, who achieved success as a result of his personal abilities winning him the favor of the king and of other high-ranking officials. Egyptian wisdom literature also emphasized the importance of respecting such men for their achievements and not despising them for their lowly origins. Yet, even if Eyre (1987a:38) is correct that ancient Egyptians believed that vertical mobility was right, both up and down the social ladder, this was almost certainly an ideal that was realized only to a very limited degree, if at all, in the lives of most Egyptians.

In order to conserve their privileges, classes tended to be endogamous in the early civilizations. Peasants married within narrow geographical limits, often the same community or even the same communal landowning group, such as the Aztec calpulli and the Peruvian ayllu. The upper classes, on the other hand, intermarried on a national and even an international scale. The Aztec rulers sought to link vassal states more closely to them by encouraging intermarriage between women belonging to the Aztec royal family and high nobility and the rulers of these states, thereby ensuring that in future generations these states would be ruled by individuals who had kinship ties to their hegemonic masters. Such marriages played a significant role in consolidating the interests of the upper classes on a geographical scale that it was impossible for the lower classes to match. These broader ties reinforced the power of the nobility in their dealings with the peasantry.

Royal kinship ties also served as a basis for integrating territorial states. In Shang China, the king appears to have married women from leading clans in many parts of his kingdom. Many of the regional rulers of the Western Chou period were patrilineal kin of the Chou king, and other local rulers tended to be related through marriage to the Chou royal family. In this way, a large region was held together by a network of kinship ties that united its rulers as members of a single large family. While this did not preclude occasional rebellions against the central government, it provided an effective basis for governing a regional state over several centuries.

On a mythical level, the rulers of the principal Yoruba states and Benin claimed descent from Oduduwa, the god who had created the world after he had climbed down from the sky at Ife. This claim provided the Yoruba states with a sense of historical and religious, as well as cultural, unity. Before 1897, parts of the bodies of the dead rulers of Benin were buried at Ife in recognition of that city's primordial sanctity. In each of these cases, kinship—real or fictional—

distinguished the ruling classes from the people over whom they ruled.

Polygyny and concubinage were common among the upper classes in the early civilizations. The Inka ruler had one chief wife, who was often his sister or half-sister. One Aztec ruler, Moctezuma II, is reported to have had two wives and, while most Egyptian pharaohs had only one *hmt nsw wrt,* or 'queen,' others were married to more than one concurrently. In addition, many rulers had harems containing hundreds or even thousands of women and produced a large number of progeny (Betzig 1986). Such behavior was imitated on a lesser scale by members of the nobility and other favored individuals. Supporting large numbers of descendants of these groups represented a potential burden for the state.

Among the Inkas, it was the custom for all of a ruler's children, except for the one who succeeded him as king, to constitute a *panaqa,* or hereditary royal kin group, whose chief duty was to care in perpetuity for the mummified body of the dead king. This group was corporately endowed with the dead king's palaces, sufficient agricultural land to support his descendants, and his personal possessions. The panaqas played a major role in the political life of the Inka state, with their individual importance depending on how well they maintained political and marital ties with the reigning monarch (Patterson 1991). In general, the descendants of more ancient kings appear to have been less well endowed and less politically powerful than were the descendants of more recent rulers. While this may have been because the older panaqas were the artificial creations of Pachakuti, the king who founded the Inka empire, it may also have been caused by the periodic reallocation of resources from older panaqas to newly founded ones (Farrington 1992).

By contrast, almost all the wealth of a Yoruba *oba,* or king, belonged to his office and hence was inherited by his successor, leaving his other children with high status but few possessions. In order to maintain their standard of living, the oba's male descendants frequently sought to integrate themselves into their mothers' patrilineal families and thereby claim a share of these families' resources. As a result, after a few generations, a dead Yoruba king had few, if any, living descendants apart from the reigning monarch and his children.

In Egypt during the Fourth Dynasty, many of the highest state offices were occupied by sons and other male relatives of the reigning pharaoh, although this practice was abandoned later in the Old Kingdom. While the rank of *p't,* or 'nobility,' as opposed to *rḥyt,* or 'commoner,' may have designated primarily the descendants of former kings, there is no evidence that these individuals were members of formal groups that had special economic privileges. In that respect, the Egyptians' treatment of the descendants of kings resembled that of the Yorubas more than it did that of the Inkas.

Administrative Control

The early civilizations were governed by bureaucracies which, although markedly limited in scope, played a major role in coordinating many different kinds of activities that were of interest to the central government. These included collecting grain taxes and market dues, administering state property, keeping state records, and supervising mining, foreign trade, state construction projects, specialized production, and defense operations. The power of rulers to control the state depended to a large degree on their ability to direct the bureaucracy that managed its affairs.

In city states, power tended to be shared at the top levels by more groups than in territorial states. Councils and other forms of consultation, as well as allocating different powers to specific groups, played an important role in the life of such states. Among the Yorubas, for example, the oba had to share power with the chief title holders of the leading lineages in his kingdom. These men collectively had the power to depose the king, just as his consent was required to confirm the appointment of any one of them. Oyo, the strongest of the Yoruba states, was governed by the king and a council of seven hereditary leaders. One of these leaders, the Basorun, commanded the army and acted as regent; hence it was in his interest to have minors on the throne.

Mesopotamian leaders appear to have possessed little, if any, more power in Early Dynastic I times than did the Yoruba rulers. Even later, the *lugals,* or 'kings,' although they commanded the army and exercised considerable control over the economy, for a long time had to share power with the leaders of the major temple corporations and the more powerful landowners in each city. Power relations appear to have varied considerably from one Mesopotamian city state to another and political arrangements within individual states often changed quickly. While kings sought to extend their control over temple lands, they were not always successful and sometimes had to abandon powers they had acquired.

The Aztec rulers gained considerable control over the calpulli leaders within the Aztec state, who were said at the time of the Spanish conquest to have had to report each day to the palace to receive their orders from fiscal officers. The Aztec king also meddled in the internal politics of allied kingdoms, but never attempted to extend direct control over the many city states that paid him tribute. Sometimes Aztec governors temporarily replaced rebellious local kings, but for the most part defeated rulers or other members of their families were left in command. The only Aztec officials that were systematically installed in conquered regions were tax collectors, whose job it was to see that the required tribute was paid according to schedule.

In territorial states, a major challenge facing the central government was to keep high-ranking officers in remote areas under control. This was sometimes done by moving them from post to post around the country at frequent intervals. Such a strategy succeeded at the cost of denying officials a chance to gain the intimate understanding of a region that could be achieved only by remaining in one place for a long time. The central government could also resort to a rudimentary division of crucial powers, such as between the military and civil administration, in order to reduce the chances of any one official being able to challenge higher authority.

The Inka bureaucracy had nine administrative levels, which extended from the king down to the humble 'ruler of ten families.' The top three levels, including that of the *toqrikey*, or 'provincial governor,' who ideally ruled over a district containing 40,000 families, were staffed by members of the Inka nobility. The middle levels were controlled by local nobility and the bottom ones by commoners. The middle and lower levels had no policy-making powers. The Inka rulers took care that these governors and local leaders did not have an opportunity to convert their positions into personal power bases from which they could threaten the control of the central government. Governors were required to report personally to the king on a regular basis and royal inspectors made frequent tours of the empire searching for signs of dishonesty and rebelliousness.

In Egypt, while there may have been considerable continuity in leadership at the village level, it is unclear what happened to the local elites after the country was unified at the beginning of the First Dynasty. There is no evidence that the rulers of the small polities that were drawn into the Egyptian state were allowed to retain control of their power bases. During the Old Kingdom, the Egyptian administration had a strongly centralized and bureaucratized character. In the course of their careers, officials held many positions which took them successively to different parts of the realm. The ideal was to climb towards an exalted position at the royal court and ultimately to be buried near the tomb of a pharaoh that they or their ancestors had served. Late in the Old Kingdom, leading officials succeeded in bringing individual provinces and an increasing range of powers under their hereditary control. While this 'feudal' type of administration is frequently blamed for the collapse of the Old Kingdom, it was retained during the Middle Kingdom until Sesostris III carried out his program of renewed centralization. While older studies of ancient Egypt stressed slow swings in the balance of power between the central government and the provinces, more recent ones have shown that significant changes were made in bureaucratic structures reign by reign or even several times by the same king (Strudwick 1985). This appears to have resulted from attempts by Egyptian rulers to retain control over the bureaucracy as political and economic circumstances, and the bureaucracy itself, kept changing.

Status Symbols

In all the early civilizations, rank was expressed in terms not only of power but also of lifestyle. The upper classes lived in more elaborate houses, wore fancier clothing and jewelry, and surrounded themselves with more luxuries and comforts than did ordinary people. While Aztec commoners were content to sacrifice quails, tortillas, maize, and flowers to their deities, the nobility sacrificed captives, cacao, exotic feathers, and jade ornaments. Yet these status symbols were always in danger of being challenged as a result of status emulation by the lower classes. Part of the authority of kings in the early civilizations was expressed in terms of their ability to protect the exclusivity of status symbols and to reserve for themselves the right to bestow the privilege of using them on their loyal followers.

Status symbols were sometimes protected by sumptuary laws, which restricted the use of prized items to the upper classes. The Aztec government carefully regulated the kinds of clothing that could be worn by different classes. Only members of the nobility were allowed to wear sandals, clothes made from imported cotton, long cloaks, and jade ornaments, or to live in houses that were made of stone and were more than one story high. As a sign of submission, no one, apart from the king and the cihuacoatl, was permitted to wear sandals inside the royal palace. Cloth that was ornamented with particular designs and colors was limited to certain classes, a specially patterned blue cloth being reserved for the king. Any man who was caught wearing clothes or ornaments above his station was subject to punishments, including the death penalty.

The Aztec kings could grant exemptions to these sumptuary laws as a reward for service to the state. Any commoner whose leg was scarred in battle was permitted to wear a long cloak, while those who had captured several prisoners were allowed to live in stone houses and wear clothes and ornaments made of gold and precious stones. The more successful warriors were, the more elaborate costumes they were authorized to wear and the more prominent were the roles assigned to them in state rituals. The granting of highly visible privileges served as an inducement for commoners to be valiant warriors and encouraged members of the hereditary nobility to emulate one another. On the other hand, a man who failed to participate in the capture of even one prisoner was not allowed to cut off the lock of hair that all youths were required to wear, so this became a lasting source of shame and humiliation for him. In these ways, Aztec kings were able to use sumptuary laws to encourage behavior that served the interests of the state and to penalize behavior that did not.

Inka sumptuary laws forbade commoners to possess many sorts of goods or even more material wealth than was deemed necessary. In Inka, as in Aztec, society luxury goods were among the most valued rewards for service. The Inka rulers monopolized the mining and smelting of precious metals and the manufacture of gold and silver objects, including all forms of personal ornaments. The precious metals that were mined throughout the empire all had to be forwarded to Cuzco and nothing manufactured from these metals was allowed to leave the capital without royal permission. Personal ornaments, cups, and dishes made of gold and silver were among the gifts that the Inka ruler presented to high-ranking officials as rewards for their loyalty and service. The Inka government also manufactured large amounts of fancy cloth (*cumbi*). It was woven by weavers who worked full time for the state and by the *aclla*, or 'Virgins of the Sun.' The Inka state collected these women in childhood from their ayllus as a form of tribute. Those who were not used for human sacrifices or distributed as concubines among members of the nobility spent the rest of their working lives serving in religious cults and weaving. High quality cloth was widely distributed by the state among members of the nobility and as rewards for special services. A peasant who performed outstandingly in the army was presented with luxury goods, special insignia, extra land, and possibly extra wives. He might also be given a minor administrative post, such as being made the leader of ten or even fifty families.

The king of Benin's regulatory powers over foreign trade gave him considerable control over luxury goods. Ivory, which was used to manufacture ornaments and ritual objects, could be obtained only with the king's permission. Although bronze and brass were worked by members of a special guild, whose workshops were not located in the palace, major bronze objects could be cast only on the king's orders. Bronze human heads, used in ancestral rituals, were produced only for the king. The casting of such objects for the altar of a deceased monarch was an important part of the installation rites of his successor. Another highly valued status item was red coral beads, which were strung into regalia for high-ranking officials. Only the king could own these beads, and he allocated them to office holders for their lifetime only. These beads had to be returned to the palace periodically for special festivals, in which the blood of a human sacrifice was poured over them to renew their power. Special cloth that was worn only by the king and high-ranking officials was woven in the palace.

Little attention has been paid to the systematic study of status symbols in ancient Egypt. Yet insignia, dress, and ornaments varied according to rank and class (Watson 1987). Some of the royal regalia were regarded as imbued with supernatural powers, and hymns were addressed to the royal crowns (Lichtheim 1973:201–2). More attention to this subject seems to be in order.

The importance of status symbols in the early civilizations made the kings' ability to control their use and bestow them on deserving followers a source of power. While too generous a distribution would depreciate the material and symbolic value of these items, the more generous a ruler could be—without diminishing his re-sources—the easier it would be for him to command the support of his followers.

Tribute

An important source of wealth for kings, especially in city-state systems, was tribute levied on conquered states. The Aztecs col-lected large amounts of food, clothing, wood, pottery, jewelry, paper, animal skins, feathers, rubber, slaves, and even a few live eagles in this manner. The amount of tribute was determined by the resources of the conquered state and the degree of loyalty it had displayed; states that had resisted or rebelled against Aztec suzerainty were taxed more heavily than those which had not. To minimize transportation costs, distant states paid their tribute in light-weight luxury goods, while nearer ones were required to deliver bulkier items. Cotton, cocoa, rubber, and rare bird feathers from the lowlands were especially valued because these items were not available in the Basin of Mexico or the surrounding highlands. Tributary states in the Basin of Mexico were also called upon to provide labor and to supply the stone and gravel needed for public construction projects in and around the Aztec capital.

Tribute goods were brought every eighty days to the Aztec capital and stored in the royal palace. In theory all these goods were the property of the king, in his capacity as the head of the Aztec state and the leader of its army. The king distributed these goods as rewards to loyal followers, office holders, and outstanding soldiers. He was also able to reward members of the nobility, valiant soldiers, and temples down to the calpulli level with grants of land in conquered states, the surplus produce of which was delivered directly to them.

The king sold surplus tribute to professional merchants in return for luxury goods that these merchants obtained from beyond the borders of the empire. Likewise, warriors who were rewarded with bundles of cloth, originally received by the king as tribute, could exchange these in the marketplace for food, clothing, and luxury goods for themselves and their families.

Tribute was also used, together with goods received as taxes, for communal purposes. Each day the Aztec king fed the hundreds of lords, guards, priests, craftsmen, pages, servants, and visitors who were present in the royal palace. Just before the annual harvest, when family food reserves were at their lowest, the king distributed food and other gifts to the poor during a major solar-calendar festival. Generosity on this scale was possible only because he controlled a major tributary network. While rulers who had to pay tribute presided over poor administrations and often had to depend on Aztec support to stay in office, the Aztec rulers and their principal allies were able to use the spoils of empire to enhance their personal power.

While we know incomparably more about the Aztec tributary system than about any other, similar relations clearly existed in other early city-state systems. In Mesopotamia, near the end of the Early Dynastic Period, Entemena, a ruler of Lagash, exacted over 10,000 metric tons of grain from the neighboring state of Umma as an indemnity for a rebellion. In addition to having to pay tribute, defeated Mesopotamian city states often were compelled to cede disputed border territory, which resulted in a considerable loss of agricultural potential. Leo Oppenheim (1964:117) has argued that "real prosperity came to a Mesopotamian city only when it had in its midst the palace of a victorious king." While an ordinary city was poor and a prey to invading armies, the sanctuaries and palaces of a dominant city were sumptuously adorned and traders, craftsmen, and retainers flocked there to serve its ruler.

Especially during the New Kingdom, the Egyptians collected tribute from neighboring peoples whom they dominated militarily. Manufactured goods appear among the items coming from Palestine and Syria and a steady supply of slaves and raw materials among the seemingly even more important goods coming from Nubia. Yet most of the gold that came from Nubia was mined by the Egyptian state, while it is unclear how much of the other goods came from parts of Nubia that were controlled by the Egyptians and how much originated beyond the borders of their empire. The economic importance of Nubia and its tight political integration into the Egyptian state are evident in the 'tribute lists' of Thutmoses III, where goods delivered to the royal treasury were recorded as taxes (*b3kw*), while the givings of individual Syrian and Palestinian princes appeared as tribute (*inw*) (Trigger 1976:110). Given the agricultural riches of Egypt and the capacity of the Egyptian kings to obtain wealth through taxation, its empire appears to have been primarily a means a defense and of securing access to exotic raw materials, rather than a major source of wealth as was the Aztec empire.

Trade

Interregional trade was conducted differently in city-state systems and territorial states. Between city states, which were often at war with one another, it occurred most effectively if traders had an arm's-length relationship with the political structures. It has been suggested that in early times the Mesopotamian traders worked as agents for temples or kings and in return received allotments of land or fixed salaries rather than seeking to profit from their activities. Yet, by the periods for which reasonable documentation is available, the Mesopotamian traders had their own guilds or associations and derived profits by selling goods at higher prices than they had paid for them. Merchants from neighboring states established relations of trust that made it possible for them to extend credit to one another and developed techniques of payment that did not require the immediate exchange of goods. Their systems of accounting foreshadowed banking techniques of later times. Such relations were strong enough even to survive wars between the traders' respective states.

Among the Aztecs and their neighbors, long-distance traders, or members of the *pochteca*, constituted separate calpullis, which differed from all but the royal ones in having no farmers as members. Trading was thus a hereditary and, except by means of personal adoption, a closed profession. Individual merchants sought to profit from their transactions and, within their own calpulli, were stratified according to age and wealth. To achieve high status among the pochteca, it was necessary for a young man to acquire wealth so that he could feast other traders and their families. Pochteca calpullis were headed by old men who, like other calpulli leaders, acted as their spokesmen in dealings with the government. Groups of long-distance traders lived in the main urban centers throughout highland Mexico and assisted each other to transact business. While they accepted commissions to buy and sell goods for kings and members of the nobility, much of their business was linked to the markets of the cities where they lived and traded.

Yoruba long-distance traders were less formally organized than were their Mesopotamian and Aztec counterparts. Many of them were women and a significant number of both sexes belonged to royal lineages. Traders often traveled in large groups accompanied by an armed escort to protect them from raiders, but each member of such a group would buy and sell goods and arrange for porters on her or his own account. They generally bought and sold their goods through local brokers, who dealt with the city markets. In many cities, guilds of leading merchants provided storage and lodging for traders from other towns and acted as agents for their wares.

In each of these three city-state systems, long-distance traders derived profits from their work and some became quite wealthy. In highland Mexico, their commercial dealings with kings and members of the nobility were a source of mutual profit. The pochtecas also enriched the state through the market taxes the government levied on the goods they sold there. The Aztec traders acted as spies for the government both within and beyond the borders of the empire, and in return the Aztec kings undertook to avenge traders who were killed by foreigners. This occasionally provided the Aztec king with an excuse for declaring war on hostile or uncooperative states.

On the other hand, relations between merchants and the Aztec military elite were colored by antagonism. The Aztecs believed that real social mobility was achieved only as a reward for outstanding military service, which implied that the profits merchants made from trade were somehow ignoble. Individual warriors proclaimed their high status openly and proudly. Yet, however rich a merchant became and however luxurious his home life was, he felt constrained to appear in public as a simple commoner, barefooted and dressed in maguey fiber clothes. Merchants could also win a certain amount of honor by sacrificing slaves that they had purchased, but only if they were also able to buy the assistance of high-ranking warriors to perform the ritual. A slave could only be sold for sacrifice after repeated charges of bad behavior had been substantiated.

In Mesopotamia, there is evidence of a similar, though less striking, ambiguity in the status of merchants. There the merchants had close commercial relations with temples and palaces, and the head of their guild or association often appears to have been granted a palace title. Yet merchants seem to have lived in the harbor area of cities, where foreigners stayed, rather than inside the city proper. They also appear to have invested their profits in land and, when they could live comfortably off such investments, abandoned trade and moved into the city (Oppenheim 1969:11). Among both the Aztecs and the Mesopotamians, it appears that close contacts with merchants in other, often hostile, communities rendered merchants suspect among their own people, thereby exacerbating the belief that their way of acquiring wealth was not as respectable as owning land or being a warrior.

Among the Yorubas, there is no evidence of such an attitude. Less of a distinction was drawn between local and long-distance trade and traders included the wives and sons of reigning kings. In towns where there were no merchants' guilds, local notables frequently acted as brokers and landlords for traders. Trading was socially more highly valued by the Yorubas than it was by the Aztecs and Mesopotamians.

In the two territorial states for which there is adequate documentation, a different situation is apparent. The Inka rulers allowed entrepreneurs to continue trading with regions beyond the borders of the empire, especially to the north. These traders were able to obtain goods that were not available within the empire, and, like the Aztec traders, provided intelligence that assisted in the expansion of Inka rule. Within the empire, however, the government appears to have deliberately discouraged interregional trade. Peasant communities moved towards greater self-sufficiency after the Inka conquest made it easier for Andean farming groups to secure land at lower altitudes, where they could grow their own tropical crops. The transport of luxury goods from one part of the Inka state to another and their distribution increasingly fell under the control of the central government.

In Egypt, foreign trade appears to have been carried out either by government officials or by traders who were controlled by the central government. Thus the government regulated the distribution within Egypt of products such as ivory, ebony, gold, and incense from the Sudan and lapis lazuli, cedar wood, and olive oil from southwestern Asia. The government also directed rock quarrying; gold mining, and turquoise extraction in the Nile Valley, the adjacent deserts, and the Sinai Peninsula. Royal workshops played a crucial role in transforming these raw materials into highly-valued luxury goods. This made the upper classes dependent on the central government for most of the luxury goods they desired, both for everyday life and to assure their well-being after death. Although, during the Old and Middle Kingdoms, the Egyptian pharaohs only sporadically obtained large quantities of booty that they could use to reward their supporters, their control over exotic raw materials constituted an equivalent source of power. The sage Ipuwer's lament, during the First Intermediate Period, that a fragmented land was no longer able to obtain the cedar wood needed to make coffins to bury the noble dead indicates how important it was to be able to provide such material (Lichtheim 1973:149–63). Natron, on the other hand, which was mixed with water for daily ablutions as well as used to embalm the dead, was brought into the Nile Valley from nearby desert areas to the west at least partly by peasant entrepreneurs.

These two examples suggest that one of the ways in which the rulers of large territorial states consolidated their power was by replacing purely entrepreneurial exchange with the government controlled acquisition and distribution of luxury goods. This helped to bolster support for the central government among the upper classes and was equivalent to the control over tribute that was exercised by the rulers of hegemonic city states. In Shang China, specific lineages are known to have engaged in trade. It is not clear, however, what relations these traders had with the state.

Monumental Architecture

In early civilizations, rulers and states expressed their power by producing monumental architecture on a vaster scale than anyone else. Elsewhere I have argued that, even in the smallest societies, human beings seek to conserve energy in activities relating to the production and distribution of food and other material necessities; therefore all human societies understand the principles of least effort and of conserving energy. Because of this, one of the most basic and universally comprehensible ways in which power can be expressed is through the conspicuous consumption of energy. Monumental architecture, as a highly visible and enduring form of consumption, plays an important role in shaping the political and economic behavior of human beings in more complex societies. This explains why, as systems based on inequality developed, monumental architecture began to loom large in the archaeological record (Trigger 1990). A related material manifestation of power was the investment of large amounts of energy in producing small, highly crafted works—such as jewelry and ceremonial vessels—often from rare and exotic materials.

The monumental architecture of the early civilizations represents a combination of engineering skill, bureaucratic management, and aesthetic qualities which indicate that more than massive labor went into creating it. Unfortunately, very little is known about the specialists who designed and supervised these projects. Zoser's vizier Imhotep may have conceived of the Step Pyramid, the first large stone structure to be built in Egypt, but more than Imhotep and large crews of masons, laborers, and bureaucrats were needed to translate his concept into reality. It is only through the study of monumental architecture from an engineering point of view that we can hope to learn more about the specialists whose knowledge and skill played such a crucial role in shaping the archaeological record of the early civilizations.

Only four basic kinds of monumental architecture are found in the early civilizations: fortifications, palaces, temples, and tombs. The last three are in effect houses for rulers, gods, and the dead. We do not find in the early civilizations the large public baths, theaters, arenas, and other specialized public buildings that were constructed in classical Greece and Rome. Even markets were usually open spaces located in front of, or between, major public buildings, rather than structures in their own right. In many early civilizations, a palace was literally called a 'king's house' (in Egyptian *pr-nsw*), a temple a 'god's house' (*hwt-ntr*) and a tomb a 'house for the dead' (*hwt-k3*, 'tomb chapel'). Yet, in extending these distinctions to all early civilizations, we risk imposing our own categories on the data. Many Maya 'temples' were built for the interment and cults of dead rulers, Inka royal palaces served as tombs for the kings who built them, and Yoruba *afins*, or 'palaces,' were cult centers and community buildings as well as the residences of kings.

Fortifications clearly had a practical function, but the scale and elaboration of many of them indicate that they were also symbolic statements. Mesopotamian and Yoruba cities were surrounded by walls. Although intercity warfare was common among the Aztecs and neighboring peoples of highland Mexico, their cities rarely possessed such fortifications and Classic Maya cities only occasionally had ramparts, such as the ones running between swamps at the north and south ends of Tikal. While this difference partly may reflect the fact that one of the major goals of warfare in highland Mexico and among the Mayas was to capture prisoners for sacrifice, the burning of temples and levying of tribute on defeated cities gave their inhabitants compelling reasons to resist conquerors. The highland Mexicans and Mayas achieved this not by building walls around their cities, but by fortifying public buildings and individual homes so that enemy forces could be resisted after they had entered a city. The massive ramparts of Early Dynastic Uruk were regarded in later times as a testimonial to the former greatness of this Mesopotamian city and their construction as the most enduring physical accomplishment of its hero–king Gilgamesh. In Mesopotamia, city walls, through their massiveness and scale, expressed the greatness of one city state compared with another. Defeated cities often were required to breach or tear down their walls as a sign of submission.

The system of border fortresses at the Second Cataract of the Nile has been described as one of the major construction projects of the Middle Kingdom, far exceeding in size and elaboration what was required for trade and defense on Egypt's southern frontier. While the final word has not been said on how great the threat to Egypt's border was at this period, the size and magnificence of these forts—as an expression of the power of the Egyptian state—must have been a major factor discouraging any challenge to Egyptian authority from the south. Hence the "hypertrophy" (Adams 1977:187–88) of these forts may have been intended to play a significant practical role.

Within territorial states, urban centers rarely appear to have been enclosed within walls, except perhaps during times of severe military threat. However, palaces, temples, and administrative centers were frequently surrounded by elaborate enclosure walls, which not only facilitated the guarding of such structures but also turned them into major expressions of the power of the central government. The original White Wall (*inb ḥḏ*), which came to symbolize the unity of Egypt, was undoubtedly a fortified palace and administrative center that, according to tradition, Menes, the founder of the First Dynasty, had established near the border between Upper and Lower Egypt after he had united the whole country. Its color was that of victorious Upper Egypt. Likewise, the rectangular wall of stamped earth dating from the Early Shang period at Chêng-chou, which measures approximately 1900 by 1700 meters, appears to have enclosed palaces and administrative buildings.

In Egypt, as well as Inka Peru and Shang China, major urban centers took the form of dispersed settlements where the elite lived in special enclaves, while cult places, burial grounds, and settlements of craftsmen, lesser functionaries, retainers, and farmers were scattered around. This dispersed pattern of settlement likely reflected the social exclusivity of the elite, who wished to avoid living in close proximity to their subjects; an exclusivity also reflected in the tendency of Egyptian kings to be buried separately even from their immediate families at various intervals in Egyptian history. This sort of settlement was possible in territorial states because there was less need for defense against external attack. The Inka fortress of Sacsahuaman, which was an important feature of the Cuzco landscape, apparently served ritual as well as defensive roles.

In territorial states, capitals also tended to shift from one place to another. This is reported to have happened on six occasions in the course of the Shang Dynasty for strategic and ritualistic reasons. The Western Chou capital also moved a number of times, particularly during the early history of the dynasty. In Egypt, the primary royal residences and burial places were located in the Memphis area during most of the Old and Middle Kingdoms, although the precise location of royal residences may have shifted from one reign to another. Even in the New Kingdom, Memphis and later Pi-Ramesses in the eastern Delta, were major centers of court life, although kings were buried and had their main cult center far to the south at Thebes. The massive remains of Akhenaton's city at Amarna indicate how quickly a new capital could be constructed on a hitherto unoccupied site if an Egyptian king wished to do so.

Although Cuzco was regarded as the center of the Andean world, Inka kings who remained away from it for long periods on military campaigns constructed 'New Cuzcos' at places such as Tomebamba in Ecuador and Inkawasi on the south coast of Peru. In these cities, as well as in major provincial capitals, streets, hills, plazas, and buildings were given the same names, and presumably served the same functions, as did their counterparts in Cuzco, even though their layouts did not necessarily bear much resemblance to one other.

In all three territorial states, kings had to spend much time traveling around their domains. This must have encouraged them to establish multiple centers where they could discharge the numerous duties connected with kingship. While capital cities were indisputably the centers of city states, the presence of the court, which was often mobile, or perhaps more precisely the presence of the king, tended to constitute the center of a territorial state.

Although temples, palaces, and tombs were the largest and most impressive buildings erected in the early civilizations, each type of structure was not equally important in all of them. Temples are generally the oldest archaeologically attested monumental buildings (Wheatley 1971). Among the Aztecs, Mesopotamians, and Mayas, they remained the most prominent public structures. In each of these societies the platforms on which the most important temples were constructed evolved into large pyramidal structures. While small temples might be erected throughout city states, the largest and most elaborate ones were located in the center of the capital. These symbolized the power and the unity of the state. Among the Aztecs and their neighbors, the capture and burning of the shrines atop its central pyramid symbolized the conquest of a state. Like the walls around Mesopotamian cities, the size and splendor of the central temple complexes in these city-state civilizations reflected the relative importance of the cities themselves.

The Inkas constructed elaborate stone temples, but they were not distinguished architecturally or in terms of central location from major palaces and administrative buildings. On the other hand, traditional Yoruba temples were relatively small structures and main state shrines were located in the more public areas of the royal palaces. The palace at Benin, whose ruler exercised more power than did neighboring Yoruba kings, contained a series of impressive compounds, each dedicated to the cult of a dead monarch. Chinese temples and ancestral shrines were also located within palace complexes. Like the other buildings in these complexes, the temples were timber beam structures covered with thatched roofs and had walls and platforms made of stamped earth. Prior to the New Kingdom, Egyptian temples appear to have been simple, often small, structures built mainly of mudbrick. Although it is clear that Egyptian kings were involved in cult activities in various parts of Egypt already in the First Dynasty, it is currently debated whether the central government was directly involved in building temples in provincial centers during the Old Kingdom (O'Connor n.d.) or whether this was left to local officials (Kemp 1989:65–66). However this question is resolved, it appears that temples were relatively less important in territorial states than they were in city states.

Palaces were constructed in all the early civilizations we have been studying, but only among the Chinese and Yorubas did they constitute the focal point of cities. Temples occupied the central position in four early civilizations, while in Cuzco the center of the politically dominant half of the city was occupied by palaces and that of the subordinate half by the main temple. Palaces generally served not only as royal residences but also as administrative centers, meeting places, storehouses, barracks, and workshops.

The Aztec, Mesopotamian, and Maya palaces were located near the center of city-state capitals, adjacent to the main temple precinct and in some cases inside it. Each successive Aztec monarch appears to have built a new palace, while leaving those of his predecessors standing. As the power of the Aztec and Mesopotamian kings increased, so too did the size of their palaces and palace staffs. It is unclear whether the Late Classic Maya rulers and their families lived entirely in the stone palace complexes adjacent to the main temples or whether these complexes were used mainly for official functions and elaborate, but less durable, domestic quarters were located nearby. Yoruba palaces occupied large walled areas, but much of their interior was forest land where the king performed various rituals.

The Inka rulers built large palaces in Cuzco, the surrounding countryside, and major centers throughout the empire. In Cuzco, a new royal palace had to be constructed at the beginning of each reign, since the palace of the previous ruler became the center of his mortuary cult. Each of the Inka palaces occupied a large rectangular block and was surrounded by a high stone wall, with only a few carefully guarded entrances leading into its interior courts. Very little is known about Egyptian palaces prior to the New Kingdom. During the New Kingdom, official palaces were located near the entrance to major state temples and residential ones on the outskirts of the capital region, as well as elsewhere throughout Egypt. Elaborate palaces also appear to have been built for specific short-term events, such as celebrating Amenhotep III's Sed festivals (O'Connor 1989).

Arrangements for royal burials were still more varied. Aztec kings were cremated and their ashes interred in small containers within the main temple pyramid of their capital city. Yoruba kings often were dismembered and different parts of their bodies buried in relatively inconspicuous graves in forested ritual centers as well as within the palace compound. Other parts of their bodies had to be ritually ingested by their successors in order for them to acquire the sacred powers of kingship. Maya kings were buried under, or close to, the large temples that were devoted to their funerary cults. A few of these tombs, most notably the burial chamber of King Pacal at Palenque, were elaborate structures. These royal burials were also accompanied by rich grave goods. Mesopotamian kings were buried within temple precincts. Some Early Dynastic rulers were interred in subterranean tombs built of brick and stone, and were accompanied by sacrificed retainers. Perhaps, like some later Mesopotamian rulers, they also constructed large mortuary chapels, resembling temples, over their graves.

The Inka rulers did not erect special tombs but, by assigning their palaces and considerable landholdings to the support of their mummies and of descendants who did not come to the throne, they diverted many resources to their funerary cults. Shang Chinese rulers were buried in huge graves dug deep into the earth, accompanied by lavish grave goods and human sacrifices. While it is unknown what kind of structures were erected over these tombs, the archaeological evidence indicates that additional human sacrifices were made there, possibly over a long period. The Egyptian pyramids of the Fourth Dynasty stand as mute evidence of the power of rulers to utilize the resources of a nation for their own glorification, as well as of the great importance ascribed to mortuary cults in Egyptian society. These pyramids also bear witness to the highly centralized administration that controlled Egypt at that time.

In general, it appears that territorial states expended more energy on the burial and funerary cults of dead monarchs than did city states. This would correlate with these rulers' control over more abundant resources and with their less nuanced claims of divinity. The Mayas are the one apparent exception. Yet they focused their main expenditure less on the burial of kings and more on the worship of their spirits in temples where they were identified with major gods. This situation more closely resembles the Egyptian royal funerary cults of the New Kingdom and those of the Khmers (Higham 1989), than it does Egyptian practices of earlier times.

The amount of energy expended on monumental architecture varied among the early civilizations. The least impressive buildings were constructed by the Yorubas and the Shang Chinese. This correlates with the decentralized political structure of the Yoruba city states and perhaps with the relatively weak integration of the Shang state. In the other early civilizations, large and durable structures were erected in both territorial and city states. In city states, there was probably more emphasis on monumental constructions that glorified the community, while in territorial states these constructions tended to glorify individual monarchs. This distinction is not, however, clear-cut. Among both the Aztecs and the Mesopotamians, palaces increased in size along with the power of their kings. The rulers of the Mayan city states seem to have erected more monumental buildings than did the less divinized heads of the city states in highland Mexico. This may in part have been because many of the smaller states in highland Mexico were as politically decentralized as were the Yoruba kingdoms.

Art

Each early civilization developed an elite art that was more formal and sophisticated than that produced by peasants in the same society. It was also so stylistically different from the elite art produced by any other early civilization that not even a casual modern observer is likely to mistake an Egyptian work of art for an Aztec or a Chinese one.

V.K. Afanasieva (1991:128) has suggested that the art produced prior to the early civilizations depicted human beings, if at all, only as integral parts of nature and that the emphasis on human figures in the art of the early civilizations reflects a new self-confidence and sense of power resulting from a greater control over nature. There is, however, no support for this as a universal generalization. Naturalistic human figures, with special emphasis on anthropomorphic deities, kings, and members of the nobility, play a major role in the elite art of the ancient Egyptians, Mesopotamians, Aztecs, and Mayas. An anthropomorphic emphasis is absent, however, from the art of the Inkas and the Shang Chinese. Chang (1983) has interpreted Shang state art as being largely inspired by shamanistic themes. Similar themes, although rendered in a very different style that focused on the depiction of human beings, also appear to have played a prominent role in Maya art (Schele and Miller 1986). The Yorubas produced naturalistic statues of rulers for cult purposes, but many of their representations, whether of human beings or of animals, were rendered in a highly abstract form. The elite art of the early civilizations tends to be thematically and iconographically, as well as stylistically, highly variable.

The art style of each civilization, which often evolved very quickly (Kemp 1989:19–63; Townsend 1979), was adopted by the different groups of craftsmen who worked in stone, metal, wood, and ivory. All of these craftsmen must have been striving to please a rich and powerful clientele which valued fine workmanship and appreciated a unified style as a concrete expression of its power and class unity. The artisans who produced these goods either sold their products on the open market, worked for members of the upper classes on commission, or were in some fashion bound to the service of wealthy patrons. When the Inka kings conquered the coastal kingdom of Chimor, which was noted for the high quality of its metallurgy, they are reported to have deported the best metallurgists to Cuzco where they became *yanaconas,* or dependents bound to the Inka state, who presumably produced goods in the Inka style. On the other hand, when the Aztec or Yoruba rulers wished to have fine works of art produced for them, they invited skilled craftsmen to work for a time at the palace and rewarded them richly for their services.

The excellence of what these artists could produce was largely determined by the wealth that purchasers or patrons were able and willing to invest in their work. When artists enjoyed the sponsorship of powerful kings, cost ceased to be a significant factor influencing the production of luxury goods. Texts from New Kingdom Egypt record that the pharaohs lavished praise and material rewards on the skilled craftsmen who decorated their tombs and carved the colossal stone statues of these monarchs. The pharaohs also supplied these workers and their families with a large support staff of gardeners, fishermen, water carriers, potters, clothes washers, and grain grinders who made their lives ones of relative ease and luxury (Eyre 1987b:173, 183). Elite craftsmen who were employed by the Egyptian state were also able to work with the most expensive raw materials and, by means of a very complex division of labor, to achieve a high degree of specialization in their work.

In Benin, the king rewarded members of the brass-smithing guild, who produced the bronzes used in the cults of deceased rulers, with slaves, cowrie-shell money, and other gifts. So that they did not have to rely only on their earnings, however, the members of this guild also possessed farms that were worked for them by dependents and slaves. While their production of major works of art was limited by the king's desire that he alone should possess such treasures, the quality of their work was maintained as the king supported a sufficient number of highly qualified specialists to produce what was needed.

It is not surprising that what many art historians have judged to be the finest art of the early civilizations was produced in the two longest-lived territorial states: the stone sculpture and relief carving of Old Kingdom Egypt and the bronze ceremonial vessels of Shang China. By comparison, the artwork of the much smaller and more decentralized Mesopotamian city states tended to be crude and amateurish, although it rapidly improved when it came under the patronage of such hegemons as the kings of the Akkadian Dynasty and of Ur III. On the other hand, sculpture and paintings of great power and originality were created in such city states as Aztec Tenochtitlan, the Yoruba ritual center of Ife, Benin, and various

Maya realms. The production of such works seems to correlate with periods of exceptional power and prosperity in these states. The fluctuating nature of hegemonic power in city-state systems may therefore explain the episodic nature of such artistic creativity.

Values and Lifestyles

Each civilization appears to have evolved an elite ideal, shared to varying degrees by the entire population, about the nature of the individual and what constituted a good life. These views made each early civilization distinct from the rest and appear to support the humanist belief that each civilization was unique. The Egyptians generalized the values of the bureaucracy. Efficiency, good manners, and the ability to remain outwardly calm in the face of severe provocations were considered keys to success and happiness. Only the ancient Egyptians are known to have deified outstanding wise men and bureaucrats (Janssen and Janssen 1990:68). Tomb reliefs also indicate that the Egyptian elite delighted in nature and the bucolic life of rural estates.

Such ideals were far removed from the Aztecs' glorification of warfare and their grim belief that the duty of human beings was to shed their blood in order to sustain the cosmic order. For the Aztecs, human life was an arduous and far from happy affair, for which human beings nevertheless had to pay dearly. The role of the individual was to serve the collectivity and the cosmos through continuous acts of self-sacrifice. While the Aztecs took pleasure in flowers, poetry, songs, and fine works of art, their enjoyment was tempered by a preoccupation with the transience of all earthly things. The somber themes of Aztec art, with its strong emphasis on death, contrasted with the Egyptians' celebration of life, both in this world and the next. The cruel forms of human sacrifice practiced by the Aztecs have caused many Egyptologists to wonder if such people can really be considered to have been civilized.

The Mesopotamians emphasized an urban-centered, commercial view of life. This led them to conceive of their deities as landowners, and human beings as serfs whose duty was to attend to their needs. The Yorubas, on the other hand, have long glorified individual aspirations, self-promotion, and rivalry, which encourage both individual and intergroup competition. These activities have inspired Yoruba praise chants and shaped their public religious rituals, which to a considerable degree focus on power struggles between different levels of government and among individual chiefs and untitled 'big men' (Apter 1992).

Specific attitudes towards life clearly influenced human behavior in the early civilizations. The ancient Egyptian bureaucrat's attitude to warfare was very different from that of the Aztec official's and this difference in turn influenced everyday life in these two civilizations. In part, these differences may reflect the specific ecological or demographic problems faced by individual civilizations. Yet this appears to explain only a small portion of the variation. That civilizations which shared a tributary form of expropriating surpluses, similar class structures, and a limited range of variations in their political organization should have evolved such distinctive attitudes towards life suggests that these outlooks—like elite art forms—were to a large degree the products either of random variation or of pre-existing, idiosyncratic cultural patterns being altered by functional constraints only to a very limited degree.

The apparent looseness of connections between these values and the basic structures of early civilizations raises the question of how far such beliefs impacted on their fundamental economic and sociopolitical organizations. Beneath their widely varying ideals, the economic and sociopolitical behavioral patterns of the various early civilizations were very similar. Whether the highest ideal of a society was for a man to be an outstanding warrior, landowner, or bureaucrat, those who were successful sought to sustain their power and luxurious lifestyles at the expense of the peasantry and manual workers. This involved them in many similar kinds of actions and promoted numerous parallel attitudes, thus accounting for the convergences we have already noted.

In this chapter and the preceding one, I have touched many times on questions of religious beliefs in these civilizations and the role they played in shaping the archaeological and epigraphic records that are their heritage. There is no way to consider the relations between beliefs and behavior without taking account of religion.

Four

Religion

When I began my comparative study of early civilizations I assumed that, because of the inflexibility of the natural laws which restrict human behavior and also because of the relative freedom of the human imagination, the greatest amount of regularity would be found in subsistence patterns and other forms of economic behavior and the most cross-cultural variation in art styles and religion. In fact, I encountered an unexpected amount of diversity in subsistence patterns, economic activities, and family organization, but a generally similar tributary relationship and class system, and only two main types of political organization. To my surprise, I also discovered a basic uniformity in the pattern of religious beliefs shared by all seven civilizations in my sample. It was only in art styles and cultural values that I found particularistic variation from one early civilization to the next.

A rather simple type of cross-cultural regularity occurs even in the realm of symbols. Elevation on a dais or throne, or being carried in a litter, are symbols of power in many parts of the world, and easily recognized as such. Kings are metaphorically identified in many cultures with the sun and with raptors such as eagles and hawks, powerful felines such as lions and jaguars, and large, aggressive herbivores, such as bulls and rams. On the other hand, it is not hard to understand why the description of a king as a grasshopper leaping up to heaven was soon abandoned in the one culture that happened to think of it (Faulkner 1969:156). Kings and nobles frequently trace their origins to strangers in order to minimize their kinship and ethnic obligations to the people they dominate (Feeley-

86

Harnik 1985; Gillespie 1989). These symbols, and others like them, are by no means universal but they provide evidence of a certain level of uniformity in the creation of metaphors and suggest ways in which thought moves along similar paths in historically unrelated cultures (Hallpike 1979:149–67).

Concepts of Deity

My most interesting discovery so far is that such regularities are even more pervasive with respect to the basic religious beliefs that are found in the early civilizations. It has long been recognized that in the early civilizations, just as in the small-scale hunter–gatherer and agricultural societies out of which they emerged, people did not draw the same distinctions that we do between the natural, the supernatural, and the social. These differences were conceived only in the first millennium B.C. by the Hebrews, Greeks, and Chinese and have been powerfully reinforced in Western societies as a result of the spread of the transcendental monotheistic religions: Islam, Judaism, and Christianity (Eisenstadt 1986). Prior to that time, the natural world was seen as suffused by supernatural energy which endowed trees, animals, rocks, and stars with reason, emotions, power, and will. This made it possible for human beings to interact socially with the natural world in the same manner as they did with powerful, and hence potentially dangerous, human beings. By placating and winning the support of the spirits that were inherent in nature, it was possible for human beings to establish a network of social relations with the supernatural that would protect and help them to prosper (Frankfort 1948; Childe 1949, 1956; Hallpike 1979). This does not mean that individuals in the early civilizations did not understand the practical operation of cause and effect as clearly as we do. No one, for example, believed that prayer was required to make water run downhill, or that such devotions could routinely make it run uphill. Yet people did believe that being able to call upon the support of the supernatural forces that were inherent in the natural world could enhance their chances of success in situations where human technological knowledge and resources were inadequate.

Early civilizations have been described as having polytheistic religions; a pejorative term dear to the hearts of evolutionary anthropologists and monotheistic theologians. This label has inhibited, rather than encouraged, a detailed understanding of the religions of the early civilizations. In such societies, deities of varying powers and authority were thought to control every aspect of natural and social life. Some of these were natural forces, others deceased ancestors, with no line clearly separating the two. Deities patronized whole societies, cities, families, crafts, and individuals. They could be related to each other as husband–wife, parent–child, or brother–sister, although that did not prevent them from competing and quarreling with one other as human beings do. The realm of the supernatural mirrored the conflicts that occurred in the natural and social worlds.

It would appear that in many of the early civilizations political struggles were expressed in religious terms rather than handled directly. While the power of the Aztec central government expanded at the expense of the older right of the calpullis to regulate their own affairs, the Aztec kings' donations of conquered land to calpulli gods helped to maintain an appearance of reciprocity between these competing levels of Aztec society. In the same manner, objections to the abuse of royal power in ancient Egypt often took the oblique form of requests that the king observe his filial duty to attend to the welfare of the cults of provincial deities (Bevan 1968:214–68).

It is unclear to what extent deities of the early civilizations were thought to be separate from one another or merely represented different facets of a holistic supernatural power. A single deity often manifested itself in the form of a human being, or in animals and natural objects such as rocks or stars. Such deities could also take up temporary residence in ritual objects, statues, and human beings, when the latter fell into trance states or were appropriately dressed as deities. Mesopotamian deities, like classical Greek ones, had distinct personalities, at least in epic poetry, so it is easy to treat them as individuals. Yet, in the earlier phases of Mesopotamian civilization, these deities appear to have been less clearly personified and more closely identified with various forces of nature (Jacobsen 1976). In at least some early civilizations, the essence of deities was believed to be the power or force behind their concrete manifestations rather than the manifestations themselves.

Ancient Egyptian deities never had very clearly defined personalities (Morenz 1973:142). Moreover, they merged with each other in a bewildering variety of ways and individual deities of lesser importance were sometimes treated as attributes of a small number of major creator gods, such as Amon, Re, and Ptah. This could be interpreted as indicating that the other gods were not so much separate creations or descendants of the creator god as more specifically defined aspects of the energy that this deity represented. This may be what the Egyptians meant when they claimed that the creator god had turned "himself into millions" (Hornung 1982:126). In the same manner, the Aztecs appear to have regarded all of their gods as emanations of the supreme deity Ometeotl, the 'Lord and Lady of Duality.' From this deity, which resided in the thirteenth and highest heaven and was comprised of every quality that existed, flowed the energy that created the universe and all that lived in it, including human beings and the various gods.

Hence it may be that, behind the multiplicity of deities that were recognized in each of the early civilizations, there was a single divine power, which united particularities such as male and female and of which the individual deities were specific expressions. In the eyes of most worshipers the question of "the one or the many" (Hornung 1982) may not have been a pressing issue, any more than medieval Christians gave much thought to whether individual statues of the Virgin Mary represented the same or separate objects of veneration (Curl 1982:38). As society grew more differentiated, so too did the supernatural.

Cosmology

In all the early civilizations, the cosmos was conceived as extraordinarily tiny, compared to modern scientific models. The earth was a flat disk, or a square, only a few hundred to a few thousand kilometers across, sometimes surrounded by an ocean. Above it were one or more celestial realms that were the home of the sun, the moon, and the stars and below the earth one or more subterranean levels through which the sun was usually thought to travel at night. The Mayas may have believed that the heavens and the underworld rotated each day, so that the night sky provided human beings with a view of the underworld and the place of the dead (Schele and Miller 1986:42). Beyond such ordered realms lay an infinite watery chaos, or nothing.

Each civilization viewed itself as being located at the center of the earthly plane, signifying its importance in terms of the scheme of creation. Most of the early civilizations also saw the world as being divided into four quarters, which were associated with the cardinal directions and to which various attributes and powers were assigned. The center constituted a fifth region, which played a privileged role in communicating between the human world and the supernatural realms above and beneath the earth. The Aztecs lauded their capital city of Tenochtitlan as being the "foundations of the heavens" (León-Portilla 1992:83). Its main temple was believed to be located at the exact point where the cosmic forces that flowed down from the heavens and up from the underworld at the four quarters of the earth came together before returning to these supernatural realms. Hence this temple, and by extension the Aztec state, stood at the center not only of the earth but also of the cosmos. The founders of the Aztec state had been led to this spot by their god Huitzilopochtli, who had revealed its identity by the presence of an eagle perched upon a cactus. The Mayas regarded every royal ancestral temple as a celestial tree which facilitated communication between the human realm and the supernatural.

The ancient Egyptians seem to have defined in more detail than any other early civilization the nature of the chaos out of which the gods and the ordered world had emerged. An endless expanse of dark, opaque, turgid water, such as had existed everywhere before the time of creation, continued to exist beyond the realm of the gods. The Egyptian universe was in fact a small bubble of divinely ordered activity (*m3't*) existing within a menacing infinity of disorder or non-existence.

The early civilizations frequently conceptualized their cosmos as being not only small but also short-lived or unstable. The Aztecs believed that successive destructions and recreations of the universe occurred at intervals of only a few hundred years. The high gods survived these cataclysms, but different ones were dominant during each successive era and the human-like beings that had existed during earlier creations survived only as animals in the next. The Aztecs were not certain when the current era, the 'Fifth Sun,' would come to an end but they believed that it would last only so long as the sun, aided by human sacrifices, remained strong enough to resist the forces that threatened the existing cosmic order. It is not certain whether the Aztecs believed that this destruction would be followed by another creation or whether the Fifth Sun represented the final ordered state of the universe.

The Mesopotamians reported that their universe had been threatened by chaos but had been saved by the invention of kingship at a time when only the gods had existed. This had provided the leadership that permitted the gods to defeat the forces of chaos, which required slaying an older generation of deities. Still later, the anger of certain gods at the noise caused by rapidly increasing numbers of human beings had resulted in the nearly complete destruction of humanity by means of a universal flood, following which the human life span and human fertility had been markedly reduced. Thereafter, not human actions but the unpredictable favor or anger which the gods directed towards individual cities and their rulers accounted for the changing fortunes of city states. A city abandoned by its patron deity could not hope to escape destruction at the hands of its enemies.

The Mayas viewed history as occurring in complex cycles of varying length, some of which took millions of years to complete. Because of these recurring cycles events were preordained to repeat themselves, so that a detailed knowledge of the past allowed educated Mayas to foretell the future. Some gods were stated to have been born on specific dates in these cycles; hence they must have died at other points. Human history was characterized by frequent reversals of fortune, which left little hope for the long-term survival of any specific political order.

The Inkas, like the Aztecs, seem to have believed that successive destructions and recreations of the universe had occurred in the remote past. Yet they saw other major transformations, such as king Pachakuti's founding of their empire, as 'cataclysms,' or transformations, that fundamentally altered the nature of the universe but did not destroy it or humanity. The Inkas defined their sacred mission as being to impose a divinely sanctioned way of life upon the peoples of the world, which required them to suppress all forms of violence and evil.

The Egyptians believed the cosmos to be especially threatened by disorder at three times—sunset, the low point in the annual cycle of the Nile, and the death of a king—but were confident that their rulers and the gods were able to overcome such threats. The Egyptians seem to have believed that the universe might eventually lapse back into chaos, which would involve even the gods dissolving into the reptilian and amphibious forms in which they had existed before they had emerged from the primeval waters at the beginning of time. Yet the Egyptians appear to have remained confident that the universe as it now existed would last for a long time.

Thorkild Jacobsen has suggested that the instability of the Mesopotamian environment was reflected in the Mesopotamians' fear of changes in divine favor, while the greater ecological stability of Egypt encouraged hope that chaos could be successfully resisted for a long time (Frankfort et al. 1949:137–40). It seems possible, however, that the cosmic insecurity of the Mesopotamians reflected to a far greater degree the political instability of their city-state system, while the Egyptians' optimism was the result of the political order which their territorial state was able to maintain over long periods (Trigger 1979).

The Aztecs and their city-state system shared to a far greater degree the insecurity and pessimism of the Mesopotamians. The Inkas, and possibly the Chinese, like the Egyptians, appear to have had greater faith in the stability of the cosmos. This contrast between the beliefs held in territorial and city states suggests that a political explanation of the differences between Egyptian and Mesopotamian attitudes may have cross-cultural applicability. But despite varying degrees of optimism and pessimism, all the early civilizations appear to have entertained doubts about either the immortality of the gods or their unequivocal willingness to help humanity. Like the inhabitants of all complex societies, those who lived in early civilizations appear to have been aware of the potentially devastating impacts of ecological or political failure and to have projected these fears into the supernatural realm.

The people who lived in the early civilizations also perceived fewer differences between themselves and their deities than do those who think in terms of monotheistic religions and of a single deity that transcends the natural world. Many gods were believed to be capable of aging and dying, being killed, or losing their power, and few of them were thought to be omniscient. Even high gods could be deceived by other deities or by clever mortals. People also believed that all human beings might share in the power that constituted the gods to varying degrees and for varying lengths of time. The Aztecs thought that by dressing kings, priests, and sacrificial victims in the costumes of deities, these people temporarily became their incarnations. Through spirit possession, even major gods could enter into the bodies of Yoruba worshipers.

That the ancient Egyptians, like the peoples of other early civilizations, did not distinguish as we do between the natural, supernatural, and social realms renders improbable Martin Bernal's (1987, 1991) efforts to trace the origins of classical Greek religion and philosophy back to Egyptian sources. It is probable that some Greek philosophers actually studied in Egypt and that certain schools of Greek philosophy were influenced by Egyptian ideas. Yet it is impossible to discover in the surviving corpus of Egyptian writings the divergent basic postulates, the skepticism, and the radical human-centeredness that predominated in classical Greek philosophy. The Greeks clearly distinguished between the natural and the supernatural, while some of their philosophers, such as the Epicureans, went so far as to reject the supernatural altogether. This separation made it possible for the natural and the supernatural to become the subject matter of science and theology respectively.

While people in the early civilizations were able to accumulate practical knowledge, because their conceptualization of the cosmos did not differentiate between the natural and the supernatural they did not conceive of natural science as we understand it. The Greeks also perceived the social realm as being separate and different from both the natural and the supernatural. Their selection of the individual human being as a fundamental object of interest implies a new vision of human beings and their relationship to the world. To make his point, Bernal is going to have to do more than propose that the real wisdom of the ancient Egyptians was oral and esoteric and therefore cannot be found in their written records or express his dissatisfaction with an evolutionary view of the development of human understandings of reality. Much as we may admire ancient Egyptian civilization, we must also acknowledge that the basic structure of Greek philosophy was different from Egyptian thought and much more like our own than was that of ancient Egypt or any other early civilization.

Humanity and the Gods

We can now proceed to examine the propositions that were held in early civilizations concerning relations between human beings and the gods. It was believed in each of these civilizations that the gods had created the world and kept it functioning. The gods had also created human beings and provided them with appropriate means to nourish and care for themselves. Through their control over nature, the gods supplied the energy which ensured that the crops would grow and that animals and human beings would reproduce themselves. Each early civilization directed much of its philosophical speculation and worship towards those elements of nature upon which its material well-being depended.

 At the head of the Aztec pantheon stood the gods Tlaloc and Huitzilopochtli, whose principal shrines were atop the main pyramid that stood at the center of the Aztec capital. Tlaloc was an ancient water god, concerned with springs, lakes, and rain clouds, and hence a vital deity for farmers in a semi-arid environment. Huitzilopochtli was the solar god whom the Aztecs viewed as being responsible for maintaining the cosmic order during the period of the Fifth Sun. In addition to helping to make the crops grow, he was the tutelary deity of the Aztec state and was closely associated with its military conquests, and hence with its prosperity, at the time of the Spanish conquest. Each day Huitzilopochtli was born at dawn, conquered his enemies—the moon and stars—crossed the sky in triumph, and then died and descended into the underworld. At the head of the Mesopotamian pantheon stood three gods representing the power inherent in the sky (En), the storm clouds (Enlil), and the waters under the earth (Enki), all deities of vital concern to a civilization that depended heavily upon irrigation agriculture and pastoralism.

The Egyptians conceptualized their physical and spiritual universe in terms of two main axes. One was an east–west axis, along which the sun moved through the sky each day from birth to death and back along which it traveled each night, either above the sky or below the earth, to be reborn the following morning. The south–north axis was traced by the Nile River, which flowed out of the primeval waters in the regions of the cataracts and back into them when it reached the Mediterranean Sea. Through their endless repetition of these cycles, the sun and the Nile River provided all the necessities of life for the people of Egypt. The east and south were regions that symbolized life and cyclical rebirth to the ancient Egyptians, while the west and north symbolized both death and the hope of life after death. The idea of survival after death was associated both with tombs, ideally constructed on the west side of the Nile Valley, and metaphorically with the never-setting circumpolar stars.

For the Mayas, the north, which was the principal direction from which rains came, was associated with life, while for the Aztecs, living in the colder and more arid highlands, the same direction was associated with cold winds and death. For all of the early civilizations, agriculture was not only their principal source of livelihood, but also the means by which the gods sustained human life. Agriculture therefore supplied the basic concepts in terms of which relations between the gods and human beings could be analyzed.

It is not particularly surprising that in the early civilizations human beings depended on supernatural forces to sustain human life. More surprising from a modern transcendental religious perspective is the proposition that human beings saw their role in the cosmic order as being to sustain the gods. While the documentation is not complete for all of the early civilizations, it appears that in most, and probably all, of these societies deities were believed to depend upon sacrificial offerings to assure their well-being. Il'yin and Diakonoff (1991:378) have likewise noted that in Vedic India "because it was believed that the world exists and that people thrive only thanks to the gods, and because the gods live by sacrificial offerings, sacrifices were the main duty of believers." This belief differs not only from the modern transcendental religions, whose deities are believed to require no human support, but also from the religions of small-scale societies, in which human dependence on the supernatural forces that animate nature is perceived greatly to outweigh those forces' dependence on human beings.

The Mesopotamians maintained that the gods had created human beings to be their servants. In order to care for their needs, these deities had to be provided with flourishing estates and with comfortable dwellings, priestly servants, food, and clothes. The Mesopotamians believed that their deities could survive without human assistance, but that human beings had been created to relieve the gods of the need to work in order to sustain themselves. They recounted that after the great flood the gods became hungry and began to repent having sanctioned the destruction of humanity. After they crowded "like flies" around the smoke of Utnapishtim's (the Mesopotamian equivalent of Noah) sacrifice, which transmitted to them the essence of food produced by human beings, they forgave the god Enki for having surreptitiously saved a small remnant of humanity to repopulate the world. A later Mesopotamian text suggests that if sacrifices were withheld, a deity could be forced to ask for them as a dog begs food from its master (Bottéro 1992:255). While we have no similar myths describing relations between Egyptians and their gods, their deities also manifested themselves in images which lived in temples, were tended by priestly servants, and were offered meals in the same fashion as was done for wealthy mortals and the illustrious dead.

The one possible exception to this pattern may be the Yorubas. Among them, sacrifice is said to have expressed the worshiper's gratitude, fulfilled vows, established communion between human beings and the gods, averted the anger of the gods, purified taboo breakers, cured epidemics, and strengthened the worshiper against enemies and evil powers (Ajisafe 1924:141–42). Moreover, the high god Olorun, the 'King of Heaven,' had no priests or temples. Yet what we have been told about Yoruba beliefs appears to have been heavily influenced by Islam and Christianity. The descriptions of rituals in which food and human blood were offered to the gods and to ancestral spirits suggest that these offerings were intended to nourish the gods. Through acts of worship, which normally involved sacrifices, the powers of individual gods were enhanced, just as the potency of egungun, or 'ancestral spirit,' masks was restored and the spirits of dead humans were called back into the human realm at grave shrines (Barber 1991:75–78).

Among the Aztecs and the Mayas, the preferred offering was human flesh to deities of the earth and blood to those of the sky. From childhood until old age, human beings ritually drew blood from various parts of their bodies and spattered it on strips of bark cloth, which they offered to the gods. Aztec priests were especially assiduous in observing such rituals. For Maya rulers, bloodletting was part of a process of seeking visions that permitted contact with their dead ancestors and the high gods. In highland Mexico, the choicest offerings were warriors who were killed in battle or taken prisoner and sacrificed. The Aztecs believed that such offerings were necessary to sustain the power of the sun and prevent the present creation from coming to an end. This mission, which was altruistic in the sense that it claimed to benefit all humanity, provided an ideological justification for the wars that created and sustained the Aztec Empire. As the empire grew, the Aztec kings offered human sacrifices on an ever increasing scale as testimonials to their power and devotion to the gods.

Despite the special emphasis that the Aztecs placed on human sacrifices, such sacrifices were offered throughout highland Mexico and everyone agreed that they were essential for maintaining not only the power of the sun but all of the other natural processes on which human life depended. If maize was the gods' primary means for sustaining human life, the strength of the gods had in turn to be sustained by sacrificing human beings. Agricultural produce and human lives were key elements in an energy flow that kept both human beings and the gods alive. Among the Maya city states, the supreme offering to the gods was the lives of kings and other members of royal lineages who were captured in battle. Such prisoners might be kept for years, until a ritually auspicious occasion occurred for offering such a sacrifice.

Among the Inkas, Shang Chinese, and Yorubas, vegetable and animal (usually domestic animal) sacrifices were routinely made to deities, as they were in Egypt and Mesopotamia. In the first three cultures, human beings were also sacrificed. While victims were killed as offerings, some were additionally used to carry messages to the gods and to dead ancestors, a custom also reported for the Aztecs. Among the Yorubas and Chinese, a large number of these victims were prisoners of war or slaves. The Inkas frequently used children collected as tribute from subject peoples. Some Inka and Yoruba sacrificial victims become deities and their burial places cult centers. Among the Aztecs, slaves who were used to impersonate deities in religious rituals increasingly were sacrificed to these gods.

Retainers, willingly or unwillingly, were slain to serve kings and high-ranking members of the nobility after death. While there is evidence of retainer sacrifice for a brief period in the early phases of Egyptian and Mesopotamian civilization, it does not appear to have survived for long in societies where human victims were not regularly sacrificed to the gods. Among the Aztecs, Mayas, and Yorubas, a few victims were killed in the course of high status funerals; among the Shang Chinese and the Inkas, the numbers rose as high as several hundred in some royal burials and included many young women. While retainer sacrifice was a form of conspicuous consumption (and thus a symbol of power for rulers), the fact that it occurred only in societies where human beings were regularly sacrificed to the gods implies the equation of rulers (or at least dead ones) and the supernatural. It is in keeping with other patterns of conspicuous consumption that retainer sacrifice occurred on a much larger scale in territorial than in city states.

The main function of sacrifice in early civilizations was to channel energy into the supernatural realms in order to sustain, animate, and propitiate deities and hence to assure supernatural support for the continuation of the natural and social orders. The fact that such offerings were believed to be as important for assuring the well-being of the supernatural powers as the support of supernatural powers was for human beings constitutes further evidence of how much more equal relations between human beings and the gods were in early civilizations than in later ones, when the gods came to be viewed as wholly transcending their creation and hence requiring no material sustenance from human beings.

Kings and Gods

Kings in early civilizations played a special role in mediating between their societies and the supernatural. Ordinary human beings had only limited contact with the supernatural, but they could sometimes request the help of deities directly, through prayers, divination, and offerings. Individual families and small communities often had patron deities or communicated with the supernatural through divinized ancestors. It has been suggested that in Shang China all of the high gods were derived from ancestral spirits (Allan 1991). Yet, while important in China and other parts of East Asia, as well as in West Africa and Peru, reliance on dead ancestors as tutelary spirits was not universal, contrary to what some evolutionary anthropologists have asserted (Friedman and Rowlands 1978). In Egypt and Mesopotamia, the spirits of such ancestors may have been occasionally requested to intercede with the gods on behalf of their living descendants, but the dead appear to have been more feared and exorcised than solicited for help. In these civilizations, individuals regularly sought to enlist gods associated with nature, rather than their dead ancestors, as their personal patron spirits.

In Mexico, each Aztec calpulli had its own temple and patron deity who was served by specially appointed priests. The Peruvian ayllus honored local spirits to whom the welfare of crops, animals, and the community itself was believed to be linked. The priests who served such deities were normally men and women who were too old for farm labor. In both civilizations land was worked communally to support such rituals.

However, despite cults at the individual, family, and community levels, relations between the human world and the supernatural one were not completely open or transparent. The king, standing at the apex of human society, constituted the most important link between human beings and the deities upon whom the welfare of society depended; relations between these two realms were mediated by rituals that only kings or their deputies could perform. A Chinese myth concerning the severance of communication between heaven and earth states that in early times all human beings had access to the supernatural world through shamanic visions. Eventually, however, the king became the chief shaman for the nation and only he or his deputies could communicate with the high god, Shang-ti (Chang 1983:44–45). Maya rulers similarly sought to enter into direct communion with gods and dead ancestors by means of trance-induced visions. It was only in the king's name that offerings were made to the gods in temples throughout Egypt, to the royal ancestors, and in theory to all of the dead in their tombs. These relations were predicated on the belief that the relations between the social and the supernatural realms, on which the welfare of both human beings as a whole and the gods depended, had to be mediated through the king.

Because of their close associations with the gods, kings were ascribed divine attributes, although the nature of these varied from one early civilization to another. The least divinized monarchs were found in Mesopotamia. There the institution of kingship was said to have descended from heaven, where it had been established by the gods. Some of the early kings were deified after death and living kings of the Akkadian and Ur III dynasties claimed divine status, writing their name after the same classificatory sign that was used to indicate a god. However, this claim failed to win lasting approval and later, more powerful kings abandoned such pretensions. Mesopotamian kings were viewed as the mortal servants of the gods, except perhaps in the course of certain rituals in which they and priests or other members of their families impersonated the gods and may have become their temporary incarnations. In Mesopotamian thought, a king seems to have enjoyed much the same position in respect to his city's deity that a foreman did in relation to an estate owner.

Mesopotamian kings might expect the favor and protection of such deities in return for their good behavior and effective conduct of their city's affairs. Yet they dreaded offending the gods, lest this favor be withdrawn. This could occur either because of personal misconduct or because the ruler had unwittingly erred in performing or failing to perform some ritual. Ironically, Mesopotamia is the only early civilization in whose legends proud or impious kings are portrayed as taunting and insulting the gods. Such behavior however, inevitably illustrated the inability of even the most ambitious mortals to oppose the power of the gods. Mesopotamian rulers sometimes sought to escape divine punishment by temporarily appointing a substitute king whose death might assuage divine anger (Bottéro 1992:138–55).

In many early civilizations, kings claimed to be descended from gods. The obas who ruled in Benin and the leading Yoruba states were descendants of Oduduwa, the deity who had descended from heaven to create the world. Aztec kings claimed descent from the god Quetzalcoatl (one of the four sons of Ometeotl) and Maya rulers likewise traced their lineages back to major deities in their pantheon. The Shang Chinese ruler appears to have viewed the supreme deity, Shang-ti, as the ancestor of the Shang royal house. The founder of the Tzu clan, to which the Shang royal family belonged, was born as the result of a mortal woman being impregnated by a swallow or a phoenix, who may have been the high god (Chang 1976:167; Allan 1991:19–56). The Inka rulers claimed that their ancestor Manco Capac, the first Inka ruler, was descended from Viracocha, the creator god, and Inti, the sun god. It is also possible that as a result of the belief that each successive pharaoh was the son of his predecessor, Egyptian rulers viewed themselves as linear descendants of the gods Re, Geb, Osiris, and Horus, who had successively ruled Egypt in earliest times. With the possible exception of the Egyptian ones, these myths proclaimed divine descent not only for the king but also for his many consanguineal relatives. All of the Aztec nobility claimed descent, through either their fathers or their mothers or both, from the first Aztec king, who was himself a descendant of Quetzalcoatl; hence all of these people were descendants of that god. The children of a vertically mobile Aztec commoner became members of the nobility if he married a woman who belonged to that class by birth.

This progressive dilution of divinity among an increasing number of people caused reigning monarchs to assert additional, more personal links to the gods. The late Shang kings apparently claimed to be the heads of the senior lineage descended from Shang-ti, which gave them the exclusive right to offer sacrifices to dead kings and to communicate through these ancestors with the high god. Each Yoruba oba was regarded as a reincarnation of the previous monarch. In Benin, this claim of divinity was maintained to the extent that it was punishable by death for anyone to say that living kings slept, ate, washed, or died.

The Yoruba, Maya, and Aztec kings were endowed with divine powers in the course of prolonged coronation rituals, which involved fasting and penance as well as being invested with regalia associated with the gods. In their coronation rites, the Aztec kings were dressed as various deities, after which they waged a war in order to demonstrate their newly acquired powers by capturing many prisoners, whose sacrifice constituted the final phase of their installation. It was claimed that, like the gods, the Aztec ruler Moctezuma II regularly had his tonalli-soul strengthened by means of prisoner sacrifices. At their funerals, Aztec kings were again, dressed in the costumes of leading gods in order to be identified with them prior to their cremation.

Many Egyptian kings specifically claimed to have been procreated by major gods, who were presumed to be present in their father's body at the time they were conceived. Under these circumstances, it was not illogical for a king to claim to be the son of more than one god. Yet the sacred status of Egyptian kings seems to have been established only during the coronation ritual which followed the entombment of the previous ruler. This sacred power was symbolized by regalia, such as crowns and royal stools, which were themselves regarded as divine. By means of the coronation rituals, the Egyptian king became the sole intermediary who could serve the gods and hence maintain the flows of energy on which the continued functioning of the cosmos depended. It has been suggested that natural catastrophes may have led to the slaying of Egyptian kings who were believed to be incapable of maintaining the cosmic order (Bell 1971).

In the early civilizations, kings varied from being the favored, if harassed, servants of the gods to entities in whom divine powers became immanent to varying degrees. Kings had to validate their powers through devotion to the gods, observing various taboos, winning battles, and sometimes performing dramatic penances. The principal role of the king in religious terms was to function as a mediator between the human realm and that of the gods. Kings claimed a privileged role in communicating with the high gods, sometimes directly and sometimes through their deceased ancestors. The rulers of Benin have been described as living vehicles for the mystical forces that ensured the vitality of the kingdom and as being able to deploy magical powers for the good of their people (Bradbury 1973:74). More specifically, kings played an essential role in the sacrificial rituals that were regarded as essential for sustaining the supernatural. Thus, whether they were considered mortal, divine, or something in between, kings were a pivotal element in the process by which human beings sustained the gods and the gods in turn sustained the natural order on which all human beings depended for their survival. For an ancient Egyptian, Inka, or Aztec ruler to claim that without his continual intervention the cosmic order would be threatened with collapse would have been a statement of precise belief, not a metaphorical boast (Shafer 1991:67). In all the early civilizations, kings were regarded as essential if not only the human realm but also the universe were to function normally.

This cosmic vision, or understanding of the nature of the universe, closely paralleled the tributary relationship on which the social organization of all the early civilizations was founded. Just as the peasants supported the upper classes by producing surplus food for them, so the people of these early civilizations provided the supernatural with surplus energy from the human realm. The peasants also recognized that, if order were not maintained in the social and cosmic realms, it would be impossible for them to produce the food on which their own survival depended. The gods and the upper classes were therefore seen as playing managerial roles that were essential for everyone. Yet it was equally the case that without the labor of the peasants, neither earthly rulers nor the gods could survive. The king mediated between the human world and the supernatural. Hence he was inferior to the high gods, but at the same time essential for ensuring the energy flows on which the survival of the universe was thought to depend.

Because of this, it is not surprising that, in every case we have examined, kingship involved a mixture of divine and mortal attributes. The New Year's rituals in Mesopotamia, which reenacted the creation of the world and the establishment of kingship, reaffirmed the parallelism between the earthly and heavenly realms (Hooke 1958). In Egypt the same word ($\underline{h}$ '*i*) referred to the appearance of the king upon his throne and the sun rising upon the eastern horizon (Redford 1967:3–27). The generational cycle in which one king succeeded another complemented the daily cycle of the sun and the annual cycle of the Nile flood. Royal succession was essential to the other cycles, because it renewed the power by which the gods and hence the universe was maintained. In an intellectual world in which kingship was believed to be deeply involved in maintaining the cosmic order, such parallels expressed what was seen as both the central ideology and the practical role of kingship.

It is tempting to suggest that in city states, where the proximity between a ruler and his subjects was greatest, the fewest divine qualities would be attributed to the king. In territorial states, where subjects might rarely even glimpse their ruler and his impact on their lives was normally mediated through many levels of government, it might have been easier to gain acquiescence to more far-reaching claims about kings possessing divine powers. This argument may be partly sustained by data from Mesopotamia, where the human nature of the ruler was clearly recognized. Among the Aztecs and the Yorubas, the ruler exhibited more of a divine nature, but in these cases he appears to have been ritually as well as physically secluded from his subjects, except during the performance of specific ceremonies. For the Aztecs, there is evidence that this seclusion increased as the power of the monarchy grew. The Maya rulers also claimed more divine attributes than did Mesopotamian ones, but their settlement patterns were more dispersed, and because of that, regular contacts between ruler and subject may have been more limited.

Among the territorial states, both the Inka and the Egyptian rulers claimed to be the sons, and possibly the earthly manifestations, of the gods. Peruvians were encouraged to believe that their rulers were the earthly counterparts of the sun god and perhaps of the creator god as well. Egyptian kings may have been viewed as divine only in the sense that their bodies, like cult images in temples, were the receptacles in which various gods could manifest themselves. But, by being in this respect potentially the incarnation of any Egyptian god, the Egyptian king became the lynch-pin that spiritually united all of the cult centers and hence the whole territory of Egypt. The Shang kings may have claimed to be the descendants, or even the earthly embodiments, of Shang-ti. But the contemporary written records are too meager and later accounts too edited by Confucian scholars for us to be sure whether that was so. It is possible that, at least prior to death, the Shang monarch, like the succeeding Western Chou ones, was viewed as essentially human. Despite such gaps in our knowledge, the available evidence does not contradict the proposition that, in general, claims of royal divinity varied according to the degree of social and geographical distance that existed between a ruler and the bulk of his subjects, and hence were more extreme in early territorial states than in city states.

As Mesopotamia was gradually united to become a territorial state, its rulers laid claim to greater divinity. Yet this process did not succeed and was soon abandoned. It thus appears that the basic Mesopotamian concept of kingship was established during the period of city states and thereafter was resistant to change, even when political conditions were radically altered. This suggests that the concepts of monarchy that formed at an early stage might persist for as long as a particular cultural tradition survived. This resembles the development of writing, which either evolved at an early stage or did not develop indigenously, and which quickly adopted basic principles that did not change significantly thereafter.

The Destiny of the Individual

Equally important for understanding the social structures of early civilizations are the views that were held concerning the origin and fate of ordinary individuals. In the sixteenth century, the Aztecs maintained that the gods had created human beings only several hundred years previously, at the beginning of the Fifth Sun. These gods had mixed their own blood with bones of people, who had lived during an earlier creation, that the god Quetzalcoatl had managed to recover from the world of the dead. The Aztecs also believed, however, that each human being came into existence on the orders of Ometeotl, the divine force that was the source of everything. In the womb, the fetus was nourished by energy that came, not from the sun, but directly from this supreme deity.

The Aztecs accepted that the principal task of human beings was to sustain the order of the universe, with little hope of their own long-term survival. At death, the life forces that were united in an individual became disaggregated. The fate of those parts of an individual that survived with some kind of identity intact depended, not on that person's conduct while alive, but on the circumstances in which she or he had died. Warriors and sacrificial victims joined the sun and, after four years, were transformed into birds and butterflies that could live eternally without working. Women who died in childbirth, after similarly attending the sun for four years, became malevolent spirits that haunted the world at night. Victims of drowning and of various diseases that caused swelling, as well as people sacrificed to fertility deities, went to join these deities in watery paradises under the earth. The vast majority of human beings who had died an ordinary death were condemned to enter the underworld, where, after four years of hardship and wandering, they reached oblivion in the lowest level.

The Mesopotamians believed that the spirits of the dead went to live in a gloomy underworld that was visited by the sun at night, but otherwise was devoid of cheer and happiness. There they were ruled by the gods of the dead and their fearful assistants. Even kings, although they were accompanied by sacrificed retainers and took steps to enhance their position after death by offering feasts and presents to the deities of the underworld, lived an etiolated existence in their lapis lazuli palaces. Human beings had been created to serve the gods and, with rare exceptions, such as Utnapishtim, who was allowed to live eternally at the edge of the world, after death their souls found themselves in an underworld that was little different from the graves in which their bodies had been buried.

The souls of the Mayas seem to have descended after death into a region of dankness and foul odors. There they were ruled by a fearsome set of deities known as the 'Lords of Death.' The souls of Maya rulers were, however, believed to be capable of outwitting the Lords of Death and escaping from the underworld by being reborn as the sun, moon, or planet Venus; that is, by becoming identified with gods associated with celestial objects that could rise into the daytime sky. Maya rulers were able to communicate with their descendants by means of vision trances. The Yorubas seem to have had a more optimistic view. They believed in reincarnation, but the cult of dead ancestors indicates that some aspect of human beings continued to survive in a separate form after death and was believed capable of influencing the welfare of their descendants.

In the Andean highlands, the bodies of the dead were mummified by freeze drying and wrapped in numerous layers of cloth garments. They were kept in caves and stone tombs where, like the gods, they received offerings and occasionally were brought out to join in religious rituals. The bodies of dead Inka rulers were kept in their palaces, where they were assiduously cared for by their descendants. Dead kings and queens were fed daily, dressed in fresh clothes, visited one another, and participated in major state rituals. They also acted as oracles and thus continued to play a role in Inka politics. In effect, the bodies of dead rulers, and to a lesser degree those of commoners, became *wacas* or objects in which supernatural power could manifest itself. Like many other gods, Manco Capac, the first Inka ruler, was venerated in the form of a stone rather than as a mummy. The Andeans clearly believed that the dead continued to exist and were capable of influencing the living.

The Shang Chinese viewed individuals as having multiple souls or life forces. While the *po*, or corporeal life force, descended into the earth with the body, eventually reaching a region called the 'Yellow Springs,' the *hun*, or ethereal soul, ascended into the heavens and became a supernatural spirit capable of helping or harming living descendants, especially patrilineally related ones. The kings and nobles worshiped these celestial spirits in special ancestral temples. In these temples, recent generations of ancestors were individually venerated, while older ones were worshiped collectively. Dead kings were consulted by means of oracles on matters ranging from major state policies, such as whether to attack a neighboring principality, to finding out which ancestral spirit was responsible for a toothache in the royal family. The royal ancestors were also asked to intercede with Shang-ti on behalf of the king. Human sacrifices appear to have been offered periodically at the royal tombs and in the ancestral temples. This suggests that the souls of at least the upper classes were believed to continue to exert a major influence over society after death.

The ancient Egyptians saw the dead achieving immortality partly by becoming integrated into the continuously self-renewing natural cycles of death and rebirth that constituted their *nḥḥ* eternity. But the dead also survived by becoming an Osiris. In this state the spirit of the deceased, living in her or his tomb, continued to be sustained by the offerings received from *k3* priests or recorded in pictures and inscriptions in the tomb. This was the *ḏt*, or static, eternity, linked to but differentiated from the cycles that renewed the universe. In these two forms, the spirits of the dead could continue to flourish until both the universe and the gods themselves lapsed back into chaos.

In general, human beings seem to have had a lower self-image of themselves in city states than in territorial ones. This correlates with the lower self-image that the inhabitants of at least some city-state systems had of themselves as servants of the gods. In territorial states, rulers generally claimed more extensive divine powers than they did in city states. It has often been assumed that the corollary of such exalted claims would be a very low evaluation of the cosmic significance of the peasant, who, in Egypt for example, was long imagined to have had no hope of personal immortality prior to the First Intermediate Period. This opinion does not correspond with what is known about peasant burials at places such as Nag˓ al-Deir, where offerings and funerary cults are evident in the Old Kingdom cemeteries (Reisner 1932). The higher image of the ruler and his fate after death may have raised rather than lowered the expectations of ordinary people.

Conclusion

The similarity of the basic structures of religious beliefs among the early civilizations, despite the cultural particularity of their expression, raises important questions. Religion can no longer be treated, if it ever was, as simply an epiphenomenal expression of social or economic relations. Yet the parallelisms between the tributary mode of production and the religious beliefs outlined above suggest that the religious thought of the early civilizations was shaped to a significant degree by the experience of life in these societies. I will briefly consider the implications of this in the concluding chapter.

Five

Postscript

I hope that the preceding observations will help to make Egyptologists and anthropologists more aware of the kinds of regularities and diversities found in early civilizations. The regularities tend to be more common at the general, structural level; the diversities at the level of specific social arrangements and beliefs. Yet there is also significant cross-cultural uniformity in the realm of symbols and more diversity than I had imagined in subsistence patterns and economic relations.

It is necessary to be aware of the broad range of alternative arrangements that are possible in the early civilizations when attempting to reconstruct the nature of life in any one of them. Without such awareness, scholars risk falling prey to preconceptions that lead them to ignore and misinterpret their data. Perhaps the most striking example of such a misconception was the widespread acceptance of Karl Wittfogel's (1957) concept of "oriental despotism." This construct, which dominated the interpretation of early civilizations in the 1950s and 1960s, was only challenged after Robert McC. Adams' (1965) detailed studies of settlement patterns in Iraq revealed that large irrigation systems in that region were a product, rather than a cause, of the state. This freed scholars to ask questions about aspects of different early civilizations that they had hitherto ignored and to formulate new theories about the development of these societies. No less insidious in its restricting influence on the study of early civilizations has been Karl Polanyi's dictum that there were no profit-oriented economic exchanges in these societies (Polanyi, Arensberg, and Pearson 1957). This misunderstanding, which it has taken much time and effort to dispel, distorted an understanding (including my own) of the economic and social organization of early civilizations for several decades.

It is clearly impossible to provide a complete picture of the range of alternative ways of organizing early civilizations, partly because it would take too long and partly because the early civilizations were highly complex. Much of the evidence that is necessary to comprehend this complexity is still missing and some categories of information may never be recovered. The rest, because of the inherent difficulties of the problems being addressed, we are only beginning to understand. Nevertheless, I hope that I have promoted some awareness of alternative ways of behavior in societies at this early stage of development.

I would like to finish by briefly considering the theoretical implications of my findings. When I began this study, I expected to discover that, because of ecological constraints, the differences in economic structures would be limited and there would be more variation in sociopolitical organization, religious beliefs, and art styles. In fact, I have found that a wide variety of economic behavior was associated with early civilizations, the one constant being the production of surpluses that the upper classes appropriated through a tributary relationship. Yet I have been able to discover only one basic form of class hierarchy, two general forms of political organization, and a single basic religious paradigm that constituted a supernatural counterpart to the tributary relationship. I have documented significant variation from one early civilization to another only in terms of art styles and cultural values. The limited variability in political organization suggests that only a few forms of political organization were adequately efficient to survive for a significant length of time.

Far from undermining my faith in a materialist analysis of human behavior, the discovery that early civilizations with differing economic and sociopolitical systems had evolved a fundamentally similar set of religious beliefs confirms this faith. Religious beliefs are linked, both in general and also in specific terms, to the central economic institution of early civilizations—the tributary relationship. This suggests that in the formulation of religious beliefs what Sahlins has called practical reason has played a far more important role than he and other cultural particularists would ascribe to it, and that, as a consequence, cultural reason, which is dominated by the idiosyncratic values of individual cultures, has played a less significant role.

To accept this position is not to deny that culturally conditioned perceptions play a significant role in shaping all forms of human behavior. Yet it raises the possibility that the nature of practical and cultural reason and of the roles they play has been misconstrued. Elsewhere I have argued that in all the early civilizations conspicuous consumption was elaborated as the deliberate violation of a universally understood principle of the conservation of energy, in order to manifest and reinforce political authority (Trigger 1990). I have also suggested that in all the early civilizations the concept of hierarchy was taken for granted as the normal condition of human life (Trigger 1985b). This attitude clearly limited what people who lived in these societies were able to conceptualize as reasonable alternatives to existing conditions. Yet the fact that this attitude developed independently in all the early civilizations suggests that it must have begun as a manifestation of practical rather than of cultural reason, which by definition is idiosyncratic to specific cultural traditions. It was clearly in everyone's interests that early civilizations should function. Therefore, consensus about the acceptable range of variation in social relations had a practical role to play in political transactions. On the other hand, once established, the belief in the rightness of hierarchy was essentially similar to the idiosyncratic constraints on human behavior that were specific to particular cultural traditions. The only difference might be that a belief in hierarchy could be more easily undermined by practical experience than could a specific religious concept, which might be reinterpreted as social conditions changed.

It would be tempting to argue in a postmodernist vein that Sahlins' dichotomy between practical and cultural reason is misleading and ought to be abandoned. That, however, is a debate which I do not wish to pursue at this point, since doing so might divert attention from another issue that is more relevant to the present study. While I do not deny that cultural traditions provide the intellectual material with which individuals and groups approach new problems, and that they therefore exert a significant role in determining the nature of cultural change, my findings indicate that practical reason plays a greater role in shaping cultural change than many postprocessual archaeologists and postmodernist anthropologists are prepared to admit. This encourages me to accord greater importance to an evolutionist analysis and less importance to a cultural particularist one than I would have done when I began my study. A particularist approach is necessary to understand many aspects of early civilizations. But it is clearly a mistake to ignore, or even to underestimate, the importance of evolutionism, as those who would privilege cultural reason would have us do.

Bibliographical Essay

Sources on the Early Civilizations

This bibliographical essay is intended to assist readers who wish to learn more about everyday life in the seven early civilizations discussed in this book. It also constitutes the factual basis on which my claims concerning individual civilizations are based. I have cited almost exclusively works that are available in the English language and books in preference to individual papers. I have also limited the bibliography to studies that in my opinion remain relevant for understanding particular early civilizations. Publications that have been superseded by more recent findings have been omitted.

Old and Middle Kingdom Egypt

The most successful Egyptological syntheses relate to political history, art history, and to a lesser degree religious beliefs. Studies dealing with 'everyday life,' although currently fashionable, tend to be popular in orientation and often lack a social science perspective. Many of them also contain numerous factual errors.

Trigger, Kemp, O'Connor, and Lloyd (1983) and Kemp (1989) are the two most ambitious attempts at writing ancient Egyptian social history. Three of the papers in the first work were written for Volume 1 of *The Cambridge History of Africa* (1982) and for this reason do not provide a balanced picture of Egypt's interactions with southwestern Asia and the Mediterranean region. Kemp's study attempts to complement traditional 'state-centered' interpretations of Egyptian social organization with a greater emphasis on individual initiative. Both books deal with the New Kingdom as well as with earlier periods. James (1984) presents an excellent picture of everyday life in the New Kingdom, although he does not attempt to describe the life cycle of individual Egyptians. Malek and Forman (1986) offer a lavishly illustrated account of life in Egypt during the Old Kingdom, but their written treatment of the subject is superficial.

Butzer (1976) provides a comprehensive account of ancient Egyptian subsistence patterns and the ecological challenges with which the ancient Egyptians had to cope. Park's (1992) recent study of ancient Egyptian floodplain agriculture stresses variability in access to water as a major factor promoting class stratification, but he may underestimate the buffering effect of low population density. Although now out of date in many respects, Kees' (1961) cultural topography is valuable for understanding the history and culture of ancient Egypt. Eyre (1987a) provides an extremely useful synthesis of what is known about the organization of labor in the Old Kingdom. This paper should be read together with Eyre's (1987b) account of labor in the New Kingdom. Edwards' (1985) study of the pyramids contains much information about Old Kingdom and Middle Kingdom engineering and organizational practices. David's (1986) examination of the Middle Kingdom royal work force is not particularly informative on this topic. On the other hand, Bierbrier's (1982) study of the New Kingdom royal tomb builders is full of information about the organization of labor and daily life.

Baer (1960) and Strudwick (1985) provide valuable studies of the changing administrative structures of the Old Kingdom. Kanawati's (1977, 1980) interpretations are more controversial, but his findings are of considerable interest. Uphill (1988) summarizes information about Egyptian towns and cities, while Fischer (1968) examines the political leadership of the provincial center at Dendera prior to the Middle Kingdom.

O'Connor (1990) examines ancient Egyptian family organization and social structure and Wenig (1969) and Watterson (1991) study the role of women in ancient Egyptian society. Despite its deceptively modest title, Wenig's book is a significant contribution to social history. Watterson's treatment of social organization is not always consistent. Watson (1987) examines clothing, Decker (1992) sports and games, and M. and J. Janssen (1990) growing up, while Manniche (1987) studies concepts of sexuality, largely on the basis of New Kingdom data. The various genres of ancient Egypt literature during the Old and Middle Kingdoms are presented by Lichtheim (1973), and for the New Kingdom in Lichtheim (1976).

Although his interpretation has become increasingly controversial, Frankfort (1948) remains the point of departure for any study of Egyptian kingship. The role of royal women in mythology and political life has been examined by Troy (1986). Major recent works dealing with Egyptian religion include Morenz (1973), Hornung (1982), and Shafer (1991). Allen (1988) presents a comprehensive account of early Egyptian cosmology.

Ancient Mesopotamia

The bulk of research on Mesopotamia in the third millennium B.C. is reported in scholarly articles published in highly specialized journals. Many of these are based on the analysis of individual cuneiform tablets. Only in recent years has a significant number of synthesizing monographs and collective works begun to appear.

The limitations of Assyriology as a field, and hence of our knowledge of ancient Mesopotamian civilization, have been considered by Oppenheim (1964). This theme has been taken up by Bottéro (1992), although in my opinion more ethnocentrically, and hence less successfully, than by Oppenheim. While Bottéro rightly stresses the need to understand Mesopotamians' behavior in terms of their perceptions and values, not ours, he is preoccupied with tracing the origins of Western science and religious beliefs in ancient Mesopotamia.

For a general history of ancient Mesopotamia, see Roux (1980). The archaeological evidence concerning the development of Mesopotamian civilization has been synthesized by Oates and Oates (1976), Redman (1978), and most recently by Nissen (1988). The most recent general synthesis of what is known about Sumerian culture is Huot (1989). This is a carefully researched and judicious work. The nearest to a comprehensive account of Sumerian civilization available in English is Kramer (1963), supplemented by Kramer (1981). Kramer's work, however, like Bottéro's, is colored by a desire to discover in Mesopotamia the origins of Western civilization. This results in Mesopotamian data being ethnocentrically interpreted to accord with Western values. Crawford (1991) offers a comprehensive survey of Sumerian civilization based mainly on archaeological evidence. The sections of Adams (1966) dealing with Mesopotamia provide a brief but valuable summary of this civilization.

Jacobsen (1982) discusses ancient Mesopotamian subsistence patterns. Adams (1981) summarizes the results of many years' research on changing settlement patterns and irrigation systems in southern Iraq from the beginnings of agriculture to modern times. His work is essential for understanding the settlement patterns and demography of the period we are considering. Walters (1970) examines the organization of irrigation projects that related to the city of Larsa and Foster (1982) the administration of institutional land during the Akkadian period.

Important Soviet contributions to understanding the economic and political structure of ancient Mesopotamia are found in two volumes edited by Diakonoff (1969, 1991), as well as in Diakonoff (1974). This work has refuted the view that the economy of Mesopotamian city states was wholly dominated by temple estates (Falkenstein 1974). Diakonoff's findings have been accepted by a growing number of Western scholars including Maisels (1990). Other papers on the economy of ancient Mesopotamia have been edited by Lipinski (1979) and Powell (1987). Snell (1982) examines accounting and pricing in ancient Mesopotamia, Yoffee (1977) the economic role of the crown in the Old Babylonian period, and Siegel (1947) slavery during the Ur III period.

Lerner (1986) discusses the position of women in Mesopotamian society and Stone (1987) evidence concerning the kinship organization of a small section of the city of Nippur. Gibson and Biggs (1987) include papers dealing with bureaucracy and Engnell (1967) examines aspects of divine kingship. Jacobsen (1976) offers the best general survey of early Mesopotamian religion, which he treats from a developmental perspective. A wide range of topics relating to early Mesopotamian culture is covered in collections of papers written by Jacobsen (1970) and Bottéro (1992).

Shang and Western Chou China

Although numerous site reports, monographs, and papers relating to ancient China have been published in the Chinese language, the literature regarding this civilization published in English is probably less abundant than that relating to any other early civilization. This literature is, however, supplemented by a number of unpublished Ph.D. dissertations.

Archaeological data relating to the early development of Chinese civilization have been expertly synthesized by Chang (1986a). A more descriptive account of archaeological data available prior to 1960 is provided by Chêng for the Shang (1960) and Chou (1963) periods. Ho (1975) discusses the long-term development of various aspects of Shang civilization.

The principal synthesis of information relating specifically to Shang civilization is Chang (1980). Hsu and Linduff (1988) summarize and discuss what is known about the Western Chou period. Wheatley (1971) examines urbanism in ancient China, although his interpretations are influenced by evolutionary preconceptions and his data are less recent than those available to Chang (1986a). Shang concepts of the supernatural are discussed by Allan (1991) and the relationship of myth and ritual to Chinese kingship by Chang (1983). Various aspects of Shang settlement, kinship, and religion are examined by Chang (1976). A variety of topics relating to the Shang period, ranging from subsistence practices to religion, are covered in volumes edited by Keightley (1983) and Chang (1986b). Keightley (1978) also assesses oracle bone texts as a source of information about Shang history and culture. Literary information relating to Western Chou political and social organization has been synthesized by Creel (1970). Granet's (1958) synthesis of ancient Chinese social organization, based on later literary sources, is of interest but is now outdated and must be used with great caution. It is comparable to reconstructions of life in ancient Egypt based mainly on records from the Ptolemaic and Roman periods (Wilkinson 1854).

The Classic Mayas

Because of major alterations in the understanding of Maya subsistence patterns and demography and rapid advances in the decipherment of Maya hieroglyphs, even relatively recent studies of Maya civilization must now be used with great caution and most older ones have become obsolete. That leaves a literature which is smaller, and in many respects narrower, than that available for any of the other early civilizations, except Shang China. The kinds of information available about these two civilizations are, moreover, very different from each other.

The cultural history of the Mayas is summarized by Coe (1987) and Blanton, Kowalewski, Feinman, and Appel (1981). The origins and collapse of Classic Maya culture are discussed in works edited by R.E.W. Adams (1977) and Culbert (1973). Current interpretations of Maya subsistence patterns are found in Harrison and Turner (1978) and Flannery (1982), as well as in some papers in Clancy and Harrison (1990). The population history of the Mayas is examined on a regional as well as a general level in Culbert and Rice (1990). Ashmore (1981) has edited papers dealing with lowland Maya settlement patterns and Wilk and Ashmore (1988) papers discussing household and community organization. Marcus (1976) examines the political organization of the Classic Maya period and papers in Culbert (1991) draw on recent hieroglyphic decipherments to examine Classic Maya political history. Schele and Friedel (1990) offer a semi-fictionalized version of the same material that is not without scholarly interest. Montmollin (1989) examines the political structure of a Maya polity in the Rosario Valley in southeastern Mexico. Schele and Miller (1986) draw upon iconography, written texts, and Maya religious beliefs to offer a new interpretation of the ideology of Classic Maya kingship. A general survey of Maya religion is provided by Carrasco (1990), while papers edited by Hanks and Rice (1989) examine Maya iconography and religious beliefs.

The Aztecs and their Neighbors

More generalizing works have been published about the Aztecs in recent years than about any other early civilization. Historical background and detailed information about settlement patterns in the Basin of Mexico are provided by Sanders, Parsons, and Santley (1979). Davies (1980) supplies a history of the Aztecs based on conventional interpretations of indigenous Mexican sources. Hodge (1984) discusses the political and social organization of small states in the Basin of Mexico immediately prior to the Spanish conquest.

The oldest comprehensive scholarly account of Aztec life that remains useful is Soustelle (1961). Soustelle was strongly influenced by Caso's (1958) views concerning the importance of 'military mysticism' as a dominant theme in Aztec culture. More recent accounts have been published by Bray (1968), Berdan (1982), Townsend (1992), and derivatively by Fagan (1984). Clendinnen's (1991) survey of Aztec life lays special emphasis on its psychological aspects and on the role of women. Adams' (1966) comparison of Aztec and Mesopotamian societies provides important insights into Aztec economic and political organization. For those interested in sixteenth-century European accounts of Aztec life, the best available in English are by Diego Durán on Aztec history (1964) and religion (1971) and the writings of Bernardino de Sahagún (1950–82), edited by Dibble and Anderson.

Aztec subsistence patterns and ecology are discussed in a number of papers edited by Wolf (1976). Hassig (1985) provides a thorough treatment of Aztec commercial activities in the early sixteenth century and of Aztec warfare (1988). Barlow (1949) presents a now somewhat dated, but still useful, survey of the extent of the Aztec empire and its tributary system. Offner (1983) studies the legal system, with special reference to the allied state of Texcoco. Ortiz de Montellano (1990) has published a major study of Aztec beliefs concerning health, nutrition, and medicine. López Austin (1988) provides a magisterial survey of Aztec concepts of the self, the human body, and the universe, which painstakingly defines the interrelations among these concepts. Zantwijk (1985) examines Aztec cosmological symbolism and its relations to Aztec social organization, a subject treated more briefly in the first half of Carrasco (1990). The symbolism of the Great Temple in the Aztec capital of Tenochtitlan is discussed by Broda, Carrasco, and Matos Moctezuma (1987). The origins of Aztec monumental art are traced by Townsend (1979). León-Portilla (1963, 1992) discusses the philosophical beliefs of the Aztecs, identifying an alternative tradition to military mysticism, and Gillespie (1989) examines Aztec concepts of history.

The Inkas

Cultural development in the Andean region is traced by Lumbreras (1974) and Keatinge (1988). Unfortunately, very little is known archaeologically about the origins of the Inka state.

The earliest modern scholarly synthesis of Inka culture is by Rowe (1944). Despite recent controversies about the nature of Inka history and kinship, it remains valuable. More recent accounts include a short book by Métraux (1965) and a more detailed one by Kendall (1973). Sixteenth-century accounts of Inka life available in English include the observations of Pedro de Cieza de León (1959) and Bernabe Cobo's accounts of Inka history (1979) and about their religion and customs (1990).

The cultural ecology of the Andean region is discussed in Masuda, Shimada, and Morris (1985). Moore (1958) and Murra (1980) discuss the economic organization of the Inka state. Various aspects of the political economy of the Inka empire are examined in Collier, Rosaldo, and Wirth (1982), Murra, Wachtel, and Revel (1986), and D'Altroy (1987). The role of women in Andean society, and how their status was adversely affected by the rise of the Inka state and the Spanish conquest, are examined by Silverblatt (1987). Zuidema advances his controversial interpretations of Inka history, social organization, landholding, and ritual behavior in two successive books (1964, 1990). His ideas about the Inka royal lineages have been significantly modified by Farrington (1992). Conrad and Demarest (1984) advance their equally controversial theory of divided royal inheritance as a cause of imperial expansion, which Farrington also rejects. Patterson (1991) discusses factionalism and alliances within the Inka royal family in the period immediately preceding the Spanish conquest. Spalding (1984) examines the impact of Inka rule on the province of Huarochirí and Salomon (1986) the impact of Inka rule upon the economy and political organization of the Quito area.

Hyslop (1984) discusses the road system that linked the Inka empire together. In another book, Hyslop (1990) examines Inka settlement planning. Gasparini and Margolies (1980) trace the rapid development of Inka state architecture from farm compound prototypes. Niles (1987) examines the social significance of different styles of house building and terrace construction in the Huatanay Valley. Morris and Thompson (1985) discuss in detail the Inka regional center of Huánuco Pampa. Urton (1981, 1990) examines Andean mythology and Inka royal myths. Ascher and Ascher (1981) report on the use of quipus.

The Yorubas and Benin

The Yorubas and the culturally closely related Edo-speaking people of Benin are the only early civilization in our sample that persists to the present. Despite the vast economic, political, and cultural changes that have transformed Nigeria into a modern nation state, many aspects of traditional Yoruba social organization, kingship, and religion continue to flourish. The archaeological evidence relating to the development of West Africa prior to European contact is synthesized by Shaw (1978) and Connah (1987). General accounts of Yoruba life are provided by Ojo (1966a), Bascom (1969), and Eades (1980). Although her work is primarily a study of the role of praise-chants in modern Yoruba society, Barber (1991) provides incomparable insights into the dynamics of traditional Yoruba social and political life. Her book should be read as an essential complement to older ethnographies. In particular, Barber stresses the individualism and competitiveness that characterize Yoruba society.

Yoruba political organization and its capacity to adapt to radical change between the seventeenth century and the end of the nineteenth century are examined by Smith (1969), Law (1977), and Akintoye (1971). Biobaku (1973) has edited an important volume which evaluates the nature and reliability of sources of information that are used for the study of Yoruba history. Ajayi and Smith (1971) examine Yoruba warfare in the nineteenth century.

Mabogunje (1962) and Krapf-Askari (1969) study Yoruba urbanism. Ojo (1966b) documents Yoruba palaces. Hodder and Ukwu (1969) discuss marketing systems among the Yorubas and the Ibos. Lloyd's (1962) monograph on Yoruba land law also provides important information about regional variations in Yoruba settlement patterns and social organization. Ajisafe (1924) documents traditional Yoruba laws and customs and Awolalu (1979) discusses Yoruba religious beliefs and sacrificial rites. Apter (1992) examines the relations between Yoruba kingship and religious beliefs and how these relate to political activity. Like Barber, he provides more dynamic insights into traditional Yoruba behavior than do most earlier studies. Valuable nineteenth-century accounts of Yoruba life are found in the travel narrative of W.H. Clarke (1972) and the Yoruba history written by the Oyo Yoruba convert to Christianity Samuel Johnson (1921).

Bradbury (1957, 1973) provides the best general accounts of Benin social organization. Egharevba (1960) has recorded a traditional history of Benin and Ryder (1969) traces changes in Benin society since the late fifteenth century. Connah (1975) reports on the archaeology of Benin and Forman, Forman, and Dark (1960) on Benin court art.

References

Adams, R.E.W., ed.
  1977. *The Origins of Maya Civilization*. Albuquerque: University of New Mexico Press.
Adams, R.N.
  1988. *The Eighth Day: Social Evolution as the Self-Organization of Energy*. Austin: University of Texas Press.
Adams, R.McC.
  1965. *Land Behind Baghdad: A History of Settlement on the Diyala Plains*. Chicago: University of Chicago Press.
  1966. *The Evolution of Urban Society: Early Mesopotamia and Prehispanic Mexico*. Chicago: Aldine.
  1981. *Heartland of Cities: Surveys of Ancient Settlement and Land Use on the Central Floodplain of the Euphrates*. Chicago: University of Chicago Press.
Adams, W.Y.
  1977. *Nubia: Corridor to Africa*. London: Lane.
Afanasieva, V.K.
  1991. "Sumerian Culture." In *Early Antiquity*. I.M. Diakonoff, ed. 124–36. Chicago: University of Chicago Press.
Ajayi, J.F.A., and Robert Smith.
  1971. *Yoruba Warfare in the Nineteenth Century*. 2nd ed. Cambridge: Cambridge University Press.
Ajisafe, A.K.
  1924. *The Laws and Customs of the Yoruba People*. London: Routledge.
Akintoye, S.A.
  1971. *Revolution and Power Politics in Yorubaland, 1840–1893*. London: Longman.

Aldred, Cyril.
  1968. *Akhenaten Pharaoh of Egypt: A New Study*. London: Thames and Hudson.
Allan, Sarah.
  1991. *The Shape of the Turtle: Myth, Art, and Cosmos in Early China*. Albany: State University of New York Press.
Allen, J.P.
  1988. *Genesis in Egypt: The Philosophy of Ancient Egyptian Creation Accounts*. New Haven: Yale Egyptological Studies, 2.
Amin, Samir.
  1976. *Unequal Development: An Essay on the Social Formations of Peripheral Capitalism*. New York: Monthly Review Press.
Apter, Andrew.
  1992. *Black Critics and Kings: The Hermeneutics of Power in Yoruba Society*. Chicago: University of Chicago Press.
Ascher, Maria, and Robert Ascher.
  1981. *Code of the Quipu: A Study in Media, Mathematics, and Culture*. Ann Arbor: University of Michigan Press.
Ashmore, Wendy, ed.
  1981. *Lowland Maya Settlement Patterns*. Albuquerque: University of New Mexico Press.
Awolalu, J.O.
  1979. *Yoruba Beliefs and Sacrificial Rites*. London: Longman.
Baer, Klaus.
  1960. *Rank and Title in the Old Kingdom: The Structure of the Egyptian Administration in the Fifth and Sixth Dynasties*. Chicago: University of Chicago Press.
Bailey, A.M., and J.R. Llobera, eds.
  1981. *The Asiatic Mode of Production: Science and Politics*. London: Routledge and Kegan Paul.
Baines, John.
  1991. "Society, Morality, and Religious Practice." In *Religion in Ancient Egypt*. B.E. Shafer, ed. 123–200. Ithaca: Cornell University Press.
Barber, Karin.
  1991. *I Could Speak Until Tomorrow: Oriki, Women, and the Past in a Yoruba Town*. Washington, D.C.: Smithsonian Institution Press.

Bard, K.A.

1987. "An Analysis of the Predynastic Cemeteries of Nagada and Armant in Terms of Social Differentiation: The Origin of the State in Predynastic Egypt." Ph.D. dissertation, University of Toronto.

1992. "Toward an Interpretation of the Role of Ideology in the Evolution of Complex Society in Egypt." *Journal of Anthropological Archaeology* 11: 1–24.

Barlow, R.H.

1949. *The Extent of the Empire of the Culhua Mexica.* Ibero-Americana, 28. Berkeley: University of California Press.

Bascom, William.

1955. "Urbanization among the Yoruba." *The American Journal of Sociology* 60: 446–54.

1969. *The Yoruba of Southwestern Nigeria.* New York: Holt, Rinehart and Winston.

Bell, Barbara.

1971. "The Dark Ages in Ancient History: I. The First Dark Age in Egypt." *American Journal of Archaeology* 75: 1–26.

Berdan, F.F.

1982. *The Aztecs of Central Mexico: An Imperial Society.* New York: Holt, Rinehart and Winston.

Bernal, Martin.

1987. *Black Athena: The Afroasiatic Roots of Classical Civilization.* Vol. 1, *The Fabrication of Ancient Greece, 1785–1985.* London: Free Association Books.

1991. *Black Athena: The Afroasiatic Roots of Classical Civilization.* Vol. 2. *The Archaeological and Documentary Evidence.* London: Free Association Books.

Betzig, L.L.

1986. *Despotism and Differential Reproduction: A Darwinian View of History.* New York: Aldine.

Bevan, Edwyn.

1968. *The House of Ptolemy: A History of Egypt under the Ptolemaic Dynasty.* Rev. ed. Chicago: Argonaut.

Bierbrier, Morris.

1982. *The Tomb-Builders of the Pharaohs.* London: British Museum Publications.

Binford, L.R.

1972. *An Archaeological Perspective*. New York: Seminar Press.

1980. "Willow Smoke and Dogs' Tails: Hunter–Gatherer Settlement Systems and Archaeological Site Formation." *American Antiquity* 45: 4–20.

1983. *In Pursuit of the Past: Decoding the Archaeological Record*. London: Thames and Hudson.

Bintliff, John, ed.

1991. *The Annales School and Archaeology*. Leicester: Leicester University Press.

Biobaku, S.O., ed.

1973. *Sources of Yoruba History*. Oxford: Oxford University Press.

Blanton, R.E., S.A. Kowalewski, G. Feinman, and J. Appel.

1981. *Ancient Mesoamerica: A Comparison of Change in Three Regions*. Cambridge: Cambridge University Press.

Bottéro, Jean.

1992. *Mesopotamia: Writing, Reasoning, and the Gods*. Chicago: University of Chicago Press.

Bradbury, R.E.

1957. *The Benin Kingdom and the Edo-Speaking Peoples of South-Western Nigeria*. London: International African Institute.

1973. *Benin Studies*. Edited by Peter Morton-Williams. London: Oxford University Press.

Bray, Warwick.

1968. *Everyday Life of the Aztecs*. New York: Dorsey.

Broda, Johanna, Davíd Carrasco, and Eduardo Matos Moctezuma.

1987. *The Great Temple of Tenochtitlan: Center and Periphery in the Aztec World*. Berkeley: University of California Press.

Brumfiel, E.M.

1991. "Weaving and Cooking: Women's Production in Aztec Mexico." In *Engendering Archaeology: Women and Prehistory*. J.M. Gero and M.W. Conkey, eds. 224–51. Oxford: Blackwell.

Butzer, K.W.

1976. *Early Hydraulic Civilization in Egypt: A Study in Cultural Ecology*. Chicago: University of Chicago Press.

Caldwell, J.R.

1959. "The New American Archeology." *Science* 129: 303–7.

Carrasco, Davíd.
1990. *Religions of Mesoamerica: Cosmovision and Ceremonial Centers.* San Francisco: Harper and Row.
Caso, Alfonso.
1958. *The Aztecs: People of the Sun.* Norman: University of Oklahoma Press.
Chang, K.C.
1962. "China." In *Courses toward Urban Life: Archaeological Considerations of Some Cultural Alternatives.* R.J. Braidwood and G.R. Willey, eds. 177–92. Chicago: Aldine.
1976. *Early Chinese Civilization: Anthropological Perspectives.* Cambridge: Harvard University Press.
1980. *Shang Civilization.* New Haven: Yale University Press.
1983. *Art, Myth, and Ritual: The Path to Political Authority in Ancient China.* Cambridge: Harvard University Press.
1986a. *The Archaeology of Ancient China.* 4th ed. New Haven: Yale University Press.
1986b. (ed.) *Studies of Shang Archaeology.* New Haven: Yale University Press.
Chêng, T.K.
1960. *Archaeology in China.* Vol. 2, *Shang China.* Cambridge: Heffer.
1963. *Archaeology in China.* Vol. 3, *Chou China.* Cambridge: Heffer.
Childe, V.G.
1934. *New Light on the Most Ancient East: The Oriental Prelude to European Prehistory.* London: Kegan Paul.
1947. *History.* London: Cobbett.
1949. *Social Worlds of Knowledge.* L.T. Hobhouse Memorial Trust Lecture, 19. London: Oxford University Press.
1950. "The Urban Revolution." *The Town Planning Review* 21: 3–17.
1956. *Society and Knowledge: The Growth of Human Traditions.* New York: Harper.
Cieza de León, Pedro de.
1959. *The Incas of Pedro de Cieza de León,* edited by V.W. von Hagen. Norman: University of Oklahoma Press.

Clancy, F.S., and P.D. Harrison, eds.
  1990. *Vision and Revision in Maya Studies.* Albuquerque: University of New Mexico Press.
Clarke, W.H.
  1972. *Travels and Explorations in Yorubaland 1854–1858,* edited by J.A. Atanda. Ibadan: Ibadan University Press.
Clendinnen, Inga.
  1991. *The Aztecs: An Interpretation.* Cambridge: Cambridge University Press.
Cobo, Bernabe.
  1979. *History of the Inca Empire.* Austin: University of Texas Press.
  1990. *Inca Religion and Customs.* Austin: University of Texas Press.
Coe, M.D.
  1987. *The Maya.* 4th ed. London: Thames and Hudson.
Cohen, M.N.
  1977. *The Food Crisis in Prehistory: Overpopulation and the Origins of Agriculture.* New Haven: Yale University Press.
Collier, G.A., R.I. Rosaldo, and J.D. Wirth, eds.
  1982. *The Inca and Aztec States, 1400–1800: Anthropology and History.* New York: Academic Press.
Connah, Graham.
  1975. *The Archaeology of Benin: Excavations and Other Researches in and around Benin City, Nigeria.* Oxford: Oxford University Press.
  1987. *African Civilizations—Precolonial Cities and States in Tropical Africa: An Archaeological Perspective.* Cambridge: Cambridge University Press.
Conrad, G.W., and A.A. Demarest.
  1984. *Religion and Empire: The Dynamics of Aztec and Inca Expansionism.* Cambridge: Cambridge University Press.
Coult, A.D., and R.W. Habenstein.
  1965. *Cross Tabulations of Murdock's World Ethnographic Sample.* Columbia: University of Missouri.
Crawford, Harriet.
  1991. *Sumer and the Sumerians.* Cambridge: Cambridge University Press.

Creel, H.C.
1970. *The Origins of Statecraft in China.* Vol. 1, *The Western Chou Empire.* Chicago: University of Chicago Press.
Crone, Patricia.
1989. *Pre-Industrial Societies.* Oxford: Blackwell.
Culbert, T.P., ed.
1973. *The Classic Maya Collapse.* Albuquerque: University of New Mexico Press.
1991. *Classic Maya Political History: Hieroglyphic and Archaeological Evidence.* Cambridge: Cambridge University Press.
Culbert, T.P., and D.S. Rice, eds.
1990. *Precolumbian Population History in the Maya Lowlands.* Albuquerque: University of New Mexico Press.
Curl, J.S.
1982. *The Egyptian Revival: An Introductory Study of a Recurring Theme in the History of Taste.* London: Allen and Unwin.
D'Altroy, T.N., ed.
1987. "Inka Ethnohistory." *Ethnohistory* 34 (1).
David, A.R.
1986. *The Pyramid Builders of Ancient Egypt: A Modern Investigation of Pharaoh's Workforce.* London: Routledge and Kegan Paul.
Davies, Nigel.
1980. *The Aztecs: A History.* Norman: University of Oklahoma Press.
Decker, Wolfgang.
1992. *Sports and Games of Ancient Egypt.* New Haven: Yale University Press.
Diakonoff, I.M.
1969. (ed.) *Ancient Mesopotamia: Socio-Economic History.* Moscow: Nauka.
1974. "Structure of Society and State in Early Dynastic Sumer." Monographs on the Ancient Near East, 1[3]. Malibu: Undena.
1991. (ed.) *Early Antiquity.* Chicago: University of Chicago Press.
Drower, M.S.
1985. *Flinders Petrie: A Life in Archaeology.* London: Gollancz.
Durán, Diego.
1964. *The Aztecs: The History of the Indies of New Spain.* New York: Orion.

1971. *Book of the Gods and Rites and The Ancient Calendar.*
Norman: University of Oklahoma Press.

Eades, J.S.
1980. *The Yoruba Today.* Cambridge: Cambridge University Press.

Edens, Christopher.
1992. "Dynamics of Trade in the Ancient Mesopotamian 'World System.'" *American Anthropologist* 94: 118–39.

Edwards, I.E.S.
1985. *The Pyramids of Egypt.* Rev. ed. Harmondsworth: Penguin.

Egharevba, Jacob.
1960. *A Short History of Benin.* Ibadan: Ibadan University Press.

Eisenstadt, S.N.
1963. *The Political Systems of Empires.* Glencoe: The Free Press.
1986. (ed.) *The Origins and Diversity of Axial Age Civilizations.*
Albany: State University of New York Press.

Engnell, Ivan.
1967. *Studies in Divine Kingship in the Ancient Near East.* Oxford: Blackwell.

Erman, Adolf.
1894. *Life in Ancient Egypt.* London: Macmillan.

Evans-Pritchard, E.E.
1962. "Anthropology and History." In *Essays in Social Anthropology,* by E.E. Evans-Pritchard. 46–65. London: Faber.

Eyre, C.J.
1987a. "Work and the Organisation of Work in the Old Kingdom."
In *Labor in the Ancient Near East.* Marvin Powell, ed. 5–47. New Haven: American Oriental Society.
1987b. "Work and the Organisation of Work in the New Kingdom." In *Labor in the Ancient Near East.* Marvin Powell, ed., 167–221. New Haven: American Oriental Society.

Fagan, B.M.
1984. *The Aztecs.* New York: Freeman.

Fairservis, W.A., Jr.
1972. "Preliminary Report on the First Two Seasons at Hierakonpolis." *Journal of the American Research Center in Egypt* 9: 7–27, 67–68.

Falkenstein, Adam.
   1974. "The Sumerian Temple City." Monographs on the Ancient Near East, 1[1]. Malibu: Undena.
Farrington, I.S.
   1992. "Ritual Geography, Settlement Patterns and the Characterization of the Provinces of the Inka Heartland." *World Archaeology* 23: 368–85.
Faulkner, R.O.
   1969. *The Ancient Egyptian Pyramid Texts, Translated into English*. Oxford: Oxford University Press.
Feeley-Harnik, Gillian.
   1985. "Issues in Divine Kingship." *Annual Review of Anthropology* 14: 273–313.
Fischer, G.H.
   1968. *Dendera in the Third Millennium B.C. down to the Theban Domination of Upper Egypt*. Locust Valley, New York: Augustin.
Flannery, K.V.
   1972. "The Cultural Evolution of Civilizations." *Annual Review of Ecology and Systematics* 3: 399–426.
   1982. (ed.) *Maya Subsistence: Studies in Memory of Dennis E. Puleston*. New York: Academic Press.
Flannery, K.V., and Joyce Marcus.
   1976. "Formative Oaxaca and the Zapotec Cosmos." *American Scientist* 64: 374–83.
Ford, C.S., ed.
   1967. *Cross-Cultural Approaches: Readings in Comparative Research*. New Haven: HRAF Press.
Forman, Werner, Bedrich Forman, and Philip Dark.
   1960. *Benin Art*. London: Hamlyn.
Foster, B.R.
   1982. *Administration and Use of Institutional Land in Sargonic Sumer*. Mesopotamia: Copenhagen Studies in Assyriology, 9. Copenhagen: Akademisk Forlag.
Frankfort, Henri.
   1948. *Kingship and the Gods: A Study of Ancient Near Eastern Religion as the Integration of Society and Nature*. Chicago: University of Chicago Press.

1956. *The Birth of Civilization in the Near East.* New York: Doubleday.

Frankfort, Henri, H.A. Frankfort, J.A. Wilson, and Thorkild Jacobsen.

1949. *Before Philosophy: The Intellectual Adventure of Ancient Man.* Harmondsworth: Penguin.

Fried, M.H.

1967. *The Evolution of Political Society: An Essay in Political Anthropology.* New York: Random House.

Friedman, Jonathan, and M.J. Rowlands.

1978. "Notes towards an Epigenetic Model of the Evolution of 'Civilisation.'" In *The Evolution of Social Systems.* J. Friedman and M.J. Rowlands, eds. 201–76. Pittsburgh: University of Pittsburgh Press.

Gasparini, Graziano, and Luise Margolies.

1980. *Inca Architecture.* Bloomington: Indiana University Press.

Geertz, Clifford.

1984. "Anti Anti-Relativism." *American Anthropologist* 86: 263–78.

Gellner, Ernest.

1982. "What is Structuralisme?" In *Theory and Explanation in Archaeology: The Southampton Conference.* Colin Renfrew, M.J. Rowlands, and B.A Segraves, eds. 97–123. New York: Academic Press.

Gibson, McGuire, and R.D. Biggs.

1987. *The Organization of Power: Aspects of Bureaucracy in the Ancient Near East.* Studies in Ancient Oriental Civilization, 46 Chicago: Oriental Institute of the University of Chicago.

Giddens, Anthony.

1981. *A Contemporary Critique of Historical Materialism.* Vol. 1, *Power, Property and the State.* London: Macmillan.

1985. *A Contemporary Critique of Historical Materialism.* Vol. 2, *The Nation-State and Violence.* Cambridge: Polity Press.

Gillespie, S.D.

1989. *The Aztec Kings: The Construction of Rulership in Mexica History.* Tucson: University of Arizona Press.

Goody, Jack.

1986. *The Logic of Writing and the Organization of Society.* Cambridge: Cambridge University Press.

Granet, Marcel.
1958. *Chinese Civilization*. New York: Meridian.
Hallpike, C.R.
1979. *The Foundations of Primitive Thought*. Oxford: Oxford University Press.
Hanks, W.F., and D.S. Rice, eds.
1989. *Word and Image in Maya Culture: Explorations in Language, Writing, and Representation*. Salt Lake City: University of Utah Press.
Harris, Marvin.
1968. *The Rise of Anthropological Theory: A History of Theories of Culture*. New York: Crowell.
1992. "Anthropology and the Theoretical and Paradigmatic Significance of the Collapse of Soviet and East European Communism." *American Anthropologist* 94: 295–305.
Harrison, P.D., and B.L. Turner II, eds.
1978. *Pre-Hispanic Maya Agriculture*. Albuquerque: University of New Mexico Press.
Hassig, Ross.
1985. *Trade, Tribute, and Transportation: The Sixteenth-Century Political Economy of the Valley of Mexico*. Norman: University of Oklahoma Press.
1988. *Aztec Warfare: Imperial Expansion and Political Control*. Norman: University of Oklahoma Press.
Heichelheim, F.M.
1958. *An Ancient Economic History*. Vol. I. Leiden: Sijthoff's.
Higham, Charles.
1989. *The Archaeology of Mainland Southeast Asia: From 10,000 B.C. to the Fall of Angkor*. Cambridge: Cambridge University Press.
Ho, Ping-ti.
1975. *The Cradle of the East: An Inquiry into the Indigenous Origins of Techniques and Ideas of Neolithic and Early Historic China, 5000–1000 B.C.* Chicago: University of Chicago Press.
Hodder, B.W., and U.I. Ukwu.
1969. *Markets in West Africa: Studies of Markets and Trade among the Yoruba and Ibo*. Ibadan: Ibadan University Press.

Hodder, Ian.

1982. *The Present Past: An Introduction to Anthropology for Archaeologists*. London: Batsford.

1986. *Reading the Past: Current Approaches to Interpretation in Archaeology*. Cambridge: Cambridge University Press.

1987a. (ed.) *Archaeology as Long-Term History*. Cambridge: Cambridge University Press.

1987b. (ed.) *The Archaeology of Contextual Meanings*. Cambridge: Cambridge University Press.

Hodge, M.G.

1984. *Aztec City-States*. Ann Arbor: University of Michigan, Memoirs of the Museum of Anthropology, 18.

Hoffman, M.A.

1979. *Egypt before the Pharaohs: The Prehistoric Foundations of Egyptian Civilization*. New York: Knopf.

Hooke, S.H., ed.

1958. *Myth, Ritual, and Kingship: Essays on the Theory and Practice of Kingship in the Ancient Near East and in Israel*. Oxford: Oxford University Press.

Hornung, Erik.

1982. *Conceptions of God in Ancient Egypt: The One and the Many*. Ithaca: Cornell University Press.

Hosler, Dorothy.

1988. "Ancient West Mexican Metallurgy: South and Central American Origins and West Mexican Transformations." *American Anthropologist* 90: 832–55.

Hsu, C.Y., and K.M. Linduff.

1988. *Western Chou Civilization*. New Haven: Yale University Press.

Hunt, R.C.

1987. "Agricultural Ecology: The Impact of the Aswan High Dam Reconsidered." *Culture and Agriculture* 31: 1–6.

Huot, J.-L.

1989. *Les Sumériens: Entre le Tigre et l'Euphrate*. Paris: Errance.

Hyslop, John.

1984. *The Inka Road System*. Orlando: Academic Press.

1990. *Inka Settlement Planning*. Austin: University of Texas Press.

Il'yin, G.F., and I.M. Diakonoff.
1991. "India, Central Asia, and Iran in the First Half of the First Millennium B.C." In *Early Antiquity*. I.M. Diakonoff, ed. 366–86. Chicago: University of Chicago Press.

Jacobsen, Thorkild.
1970. *Toward the Image of Tammuz and Other Essays on Mesopotamian History and Culture*. Cambridge: Harvard University Press.
1976. *The Treasures of Darkness: A History of Mesopotamian Religion*. New Haven: Yale University Press.
1982. *Salinity and Irrigation Agriculture in Antiquity: Diyala Basin Archaeological Projects: Report on Essential Results, 1956–58*. Malibu: Undena.

James, T.G.H.
1962. *The Hekanakhte Papers and Other Early Middle Kingdom Documents*. Publications of the Metropolitan Museum of Art Egyptian Expedition, 19. New York: Metropolitan Museum of Art.
1984. *Pharaoh's People: Scenes from Life in Imperial Egypt*. Chicago: University of Chicago Press.

Janssen, R.M., and J.J. Janssen.
1990. *Growing Up in Ancient Egypt*. London: Rubicon.

Johnson, G.A.
1973. *Local Exchange and Early State Development in Southwestern Iran*. Ann Arbor: University of Michigan, Museum of Anthropology, Anthropological Papers, 51.

Johnson, Samuel.
1921. *The History of the Yorubas from the Earliest Times to the Beginning of the British Protectorate*. Edited by O. Johnson. London: Routledge.

Jones, G.D., and R.R. Kautz, eds.
1981. *The Transition to Statehood in the New World*. Cambridge: Cambridge University Press.

Jorgensen, J.G., ed.
1974. *Comparative Studies by Harold E. Driver and Essays in his Honor*. New Haven: HRAF Press.

Kanawati, Naguib.
1977. *The Egyptian Administration in the Old Kingdom: Evidence on Its Economic Decline*. Warminster: Aris and Phillips.

1980. *Governmental Reforms in Old Kingdom Egypt.* Warminster: Aris and Phillips.

Keatinge, R.W.

1988. *Peruvian Prehistory: An Overview of Pre-Inca and Inca Society.* Cambridge: Cambridge University Press.

Kees, Hermann.

1961. *Ancient Egypt: A Cultural Topography.* Chicago: University of Chicago Press.

Keightley, D.N.

1978. *Sources of Shang History: The Oracle-Bone Inscriptions of Bronze Age China.* Berkeley: University of California Press.

1983. (ed.) *The Origins of Chinese Civilization.* Berkeley: University of California Press.

Kemp, B.J.

1989. *Ancient Egypt: Anatomy of a Civilization.* London: Routledge.

Kendall, Ann.

1973. *Everyday Life of the Incas.* London: Batsford.

Köbben, A.J.F.

1952. "New Ways of Presenting an Old Idea: The Statistical Method in Social Anthropology." *The Journal of the Royal Anthropological Institute* 82: 129–46.

1973. "Comparativists and Non-Comparativists in Anthropology." In *A Handbook of Method in Cultural Anthropology.* Raoul Naroll and Ronald Cohen, eds. 581–96. New York: Columbia University Press.

Kramer, S.N.

1963. *The Sumerians: Their History, Culture, and Character.* Chicago: University of Chicago Press.

1981. *History Begins at Sumer: Thirty-nine Firsts in Man's Recorded History.* 3rd rev. ed. Philadelphia: University of Pennsylvania Press.

Krapf-Askari, Eva.

1969. *Yoruba Towns and Cities: An Enquiry into the Nature of Urban Social Phenomena.* Oxford: Oxford University Press.

Law, Robin.

1977. *The Oyo Empire, c. 1600–c.1836: A West African Imperialism in the Era of the Atlantic Slave Trade.* Oxford: Oxford University Press.

León-Portilla, Miguel.

1963. *Aztec Thought and Culture: A Study of the Ancient Nahuatl Mind.* Norman: University of Oklahoma Press.

1992. *The Aztec Image of Self and Society: An Introduction to Nahua Culture.* Salt Lake City: University of Utah Press.

Lerner, Gerda.

1986. *The Creation of Patriarchy.* New York: Oxford University Press.

Lichtheim, Miriam.

1973. *Ancient Egyptian Literature: A Book of Readings.* Vol. 1, *The Old and Middle Kingdoms.* Berkeley: University of California Press.

1976. *Ancient Egyptian Literature: A Book of Readings.* Vol. 2, *The New Kingdom.* Berkeley: University of California Press.

Lipinski, Edward, ed.

1979. *State and Temple Economy in the Ancient Near East.* Leuven: Departement Oriëntalistiek, Katholieke Universiteit Leuven.

Lloyd, P.C.

1962. *Yoruba Land Law.* London: Oxford University Press.

López Austin, Alfredo.

1988. *The Human Body and Ideology: Concepts of the Ancient Nahuas.* 2 vols. Salt Lake City: University of Utah Press.

Lumbreras, L.G.

1974. *The Peoples and Cultures of Ancient Peru.* Washington, D.C.: Smithsonian Institution Press.

McNeill, W.H.

1976. *Plagues and Peoples.* Garden City, New York: Anchor.

Mabogunje, A.L.

1962. *Yoruba Towns.* Ibadan: Ibadan University Press.

Maisels, C.K.

1990. *The Emergence of Civilization: From Hunting and Gathering to Agriculture, Cities, and the State in the Near East.* London: Routledge.

Malek, Jaromir, and Werner Forman.

1986. *In the Shadow of the Pyramids: Egypt during the Old Kingdom.* Norman: University of Oklahoma Press.

Manniche, Lise.

1987. *Sexual Life in Ancient Egypt.* London: KPI.

Marcus, Joyce.
  1976. *Emblem and State in the Classic Maya Lowlands*. Washington, D.C.: Dumbarton Oaks.
Marx, Karl.
  1964. *Pre-capitalist Economic Formations*. E.J. Hobsbawm, ed. London: Lawrence and Wishart.
Masuda, Shozo, Izumi Shimada, and Craig Morris, eds.
  1985. *Andean Ecology and Civilization: An Interdisciplinary Perspective on Andean Ecological Complementarity*. Tokyo: University of Tokyo Press.
Métraux, Alfred.
  1965. *The Incas*. London: Studio Vista.
Montmollin, Olivier de.
  1989. *The Archaeology of Political Structure: Settlement Analysis in a Classic Maya Polity*. Cambridge: Cambridge University Press.
Moore, F.W., ed.
  1961. *Readings in Cross-Cultural Methodology*. New Haven: HRAF Press.
Moore, S.F.
  1958. *Power and Property in Inca Peru*. New York: Columbia University Press.
Morenz, Siegfried.
  1973. *Egyptian Religion*. Ithaca: Cornell University Press.
Morgan, L.H.
  1907. *Ancient Society; or, Researches in the Lines of Human Progress from Savagery through Barbarism to Civilization*. Chicago: Kerr. (originally published in 1877).
Morris, Craig, and D.E. Thompson.
  1985. *Huánuco Pampa: An Inca City and Its Hinterland*. London: Thames and Hudson.
Murdock, G.P.
  1959. "Evolution in Social Organization." In *Evolution and Anthropology: A Centennial Appraisal*. B.J. Meggers, ed. 126–43. Washington, D.C.: Anthropological Society of Washington.
  1981. *Atlas of World Cultures*. Pittsburgh: University of Pittsburgh Press.

Murra, J.V.

1980. *The Economic Organization of the Inka State.* Greenwich, Connecticut: JAI Press.

Murra, J.V., Nathan Wachtel, and Jacques Revel, eds.

1986. *Anthropological History of Andean Polities.* Cambridge: Cambridge University Press.

Netting, R.McC.

1969. "Ecosystems in Process: A Comparative Study of Change in Two West African Societies." In *Contributions to Anthropology: Ecological Essays.* David Damas, ed. 102–12. Ottawa: National Museums of Canada, Bulletin 230.

Niles, S.A.

1987. *Callachaca: Style and Status in an Inca Community.* Iowa City: University of Iowa Press.

Nissen, H.J.

1988. *The Early History of the Ancient Near East, 9000–2000 B.C.* Chicago: University of Chicago Press.

Oates, David, and Joan Oates.

1976. *The Rise of Civilization.* Oxford: Elsevier-Phaidon.

O'Connor, David.

1989. "City and Palace in New Kingdom Egypt." Cahier de Recherches de l'Institut de Papyrologie et d'Egyptologie de Lille 11: 73–87.

1990. *Ancient Egyptian Society.* Pittsburgh: The Carnegie Museum of Natural History.

n.d. "The Status of Early Egyptian Temples: An Alternative Theory." In *The Followers of Horus: Studies in Memory of Michael Alan Hoffman.* B. Adams and R. Friedman, eds. Oxford: Oxbow (in press).

Offner, J.A.

1983. *Law and Politics in Aztec Texcoco.* Cambridge: Cambridge University Press.

Ojo, G.J.A.

1966a. *Yoruba Culture: A Geographical Analysis.* London: University of London Press.

1966b. *Yoruba Palaces: A Study of Afins of Yorubaland.* London: University of London Press.

Oppenheim, A.L.

1964. *Ancient Mesopotamia: Portrait of a Dead Civilization.* Chicago: University of Chicago Press.

1969. "Mesopotamia—Land of Many Cities." In *Middle Eastern Cities: A Symposium on Ancient, Islamic, and Contemporary Middle Eastern Urbanism.* I.M. Lapidus, ed. 3–18. Berkeley: University of California Press.

Ortiz de Montellano, Bernard.

1990. *Aztec Medicine, Health, and Nutrition.* Rutgers: Rutgers University Press.

Park, T.K.

1992. "Early Trends Toward Class Stratification: Chaos, Common Property, and Flood Recession Agriculture." *American Anthropologist* 94: 90–117.

Patterson, T.C.

1991. *The Inca Empire: The Formation and Disintegration of a Pre-Capitalist State.* New York: St. Martin's.

Polanyi, Karl, C.M. Arensberg, and H.W. Pearson.

1957. *Trade and Market in the Early Empires.* Glencoe: Free Press.

Powell, Marvin, ed.

1987. *Labor in the Ancient Near East.* American Oriental Series, 68. New Haven: American Oriental Society.

Preucel, R.W., ed.

1991. *Processual and Postprocessual Archaeologies: Multiple Ways of Knowing the Past.* Carbondale: Southern Illinois University at Carbondale, Center for Archaeological Investigations. Occasional Paper, 10.

Redford, D.B.

1967. *History and Chronology of the Eighteenth Dynasty of Egypt.* Toronto: University of Toronto Press.

Redman, C.L.

1978. *The Rise of Civilization from Early Farmers to Urban Society in the Ancient Near East.* San Francisco: Freeman.

Reisner, G.A.

1932. *A Provincial Cemetery of the Pyramid Age, Naga-ed-Dêr.* Berkeley: University of California Press.

Robertshaw, Peter, ed.
   1990. *A History of African Archaeology.* London: Currey.
Roux, Georges.
   1980. *Ancient Iraq.* 2nd ed. Harmondsworth: Penguin.
Rowe, J.H.
   1944. "Inca Culture at the Time of the Spanish Conquest." In *Handbook of South American Indians.* Vol. 2, *The Andean Civilizations.* J.H. Steward, ed. 183–330. Washington, D.C.: Smithsonian Institution, Bureau of American Ethnology, Bulletin 143.
Ryder, A.F.C.
   1969. *Benin and the Europeans, 1485–1897.* London: Longmans.
Sahagún, Pernardino de.
   1950–82 *Florentine Codex: General History of the Things of New Spain.* 13 Vols. A.J.O. Anderson and C.E. Dibble, eds. Santa Fe: School of American Research and Salt Lake City: University of Utah Press.
Sahlins, M.D.
   1976. *Culture and Practical Reason.* Chicago: University of Chicago Press.
Salomon, Frank.
   1986. *Native Lords of Quito in the Age of the Incas: The Political Economy of North-Andean Chiefdoms.* Cambridge: Cambridge University Press.
Sanders, W.T., J.R. Parsons, and R.S. Santley.
   1979. *The Basin of Mexico: Ecological Processes in the Evolution of a Civilization.* New York: Academic Press.
Schele, Linda, and David Freidel.
   1990. *A Forest of Kings: The Untold Story of the Ancient Maya.* New York: Morrow.
Schele, Linda, and M.E. Miller.
   1986. *The Blood of Kings: Dynasty and Ritual in Maya Art.* New York: Braziller.
Service, E.R.
   1971. *Primitive Social Organization: An Evolutionary Perspective.* 2nd ed. New York: Random House.

1975. *Origins of the State and Civilization: The Process of Cultural Evolution.* New York: Norton.

Shafer, B.E., ed.
1991. *Religion in Ancient Egypt: Gods, Myths, and Personal Practice.* Ithaca: Cornell University Press.

Shanks, Michael, and Christopher Tilley.
1987. *Social Theory and Archaeology.* Cambridge: Polity Press.

Shaw, Thurstan.
1978. *Nigeria: Its Archaeology and Early History.* London: Thames and Hudson.

Siegel, B.J.
1947. *Slavery during the Third Dynasty of Ur.* Menasha: American Anthropological Association, Memoir 66.

Silverblatt, Irene.
1987. *Moon, Sun, and Witches: Gender Ideologies and Class in Inca and Colonial Peru.* Princeton: Princeton University Press.

Sioui, Georges.
1992. *For an Amerindian Autohistory: An Essay on the Foundations of a Social Ethic.* Montreal: McGill-Queen's University Press.

Sjoberg, Gideon.
1960. *The Preindustrial City: Past and Present.* Glencoe: The Free Press.

Smith, Robert.
1969. *Kingdoms of the Yoruba.* London: Methuen.

Snell, Daniel.
1982. *Ledgers and Prices: Early Mesopotamian Merchant Accounts.* New Haven: Yale University Press.

Soustelle, Jacques.
1961. *The Daily Life of the Aztecs on the Eve of the Spanish Conquest.* New York: Macmillan.

Spalding, Karen.
1984. *Huarochirí: An Andean Society under Inca and Spanish Rule.* Stanford: Stanford University Press.

Steward, J.H.
1949. "Cultural Causality and Law: A Trial Formulation of the Development of Early Civilizations." *American Anthropologist* 51: 1–27.

Stone, E.C.
   1987. *Nippur Neighborhoods*. Studies in Ancient Oriental Civili-
   zation, 44. Chicago: Oriental Institute of the University of Chicago.
Strudwick, Nigel.
   1985. *The Administration of Egypt in the Old Kingdom: The
   Highest Titles and their Holders*. London: KPI.
Tainter, J.A.
   1988. *The Collapse of Complex Societies*. Cambridge: Cambridge
   University Press.
Textor, R.B., comp.
   1967. *A Cross-Cultural Summary*. New Haven: HRAF Press.
Townsend, R.F.
   1979. *State and Cosmos in the Art of Tenochtitlan*. Studies in Pre-
   Columbian Art and Archaeology, 20. Washington, D.C.:
   Dumbarton Oaks.
   1992. *The Aztecs*. London: Thames and Hudson.
Trigger, B.G.
   1976. *Nubia under the Pharaohs*. London: Thames and Hudson.
   1979. "Egypt and the Comparative Study of Early Civilizations."
   In *Egyptology and the Social Sciences: Five Studies*. K.R. Weeks,
   ed. 23–56. Cairo: American University in Cairo Press.
   1985a. "The Evolution of Pre-Industrial Cities: A Multilinear
   Perspective." In *Mélanges offerts à Jean Vercoutter*. Francis
   Geus and Florence Thill, eds. 343–53. Paris: Editions Recherche
   sur les Civilisations.
   1985b. "Generalized Coercion and Inequality: The Basis of State
   Power in the Early Civilizations." In *Development and Decline:
   The Evolution of Sociopolitical Organization*. H.J. Claessen,
   Pieter van de Velde, and M.E. Smith, eds. 46–61. South Hadley,
   Massachusetts: Bergin and Garvey.
   1990. "Monumental Architecture: A Thermodynamic Explana-
   tion of Symbolic Behavior." *World Archaeology* 22: 119–32.
Trigger, B.G., B.J. Kemp, D. O'Connor, and A.B. Lloyd.
   1983. *Ancient Egypt: A Social History*. Cambridge: Cambridge
   University Press.
Troy, Lana.
   1986. *Patterns of Queenship in Ancient Egyptian Myth and His-*

tory. Uppsala: Boreas, Uppsala Studies in Ancient Mediterranean and Near Eastern Civilizations, 14.

Turner, Victor.

1967. *The Forest of Symbols: Aspects of Ndembu Ritual*. Ithaca: Cornell University Press.

1975. *Revelation and Divination in Ndembu Ritual*. Ithaca: Cornell University Press.

Uphill, E.P.

1988. *Egyptian Towns and Cities*. Aylesbury: Shire Publications.

Urton, Gary.

1981. *At the Crossroads of the Earth and the Sky: An Andean Cosmology*. Austin: University of Texas Press.

1990. *The History of a Myth: Pacariqtambo and the Origin of the Inkas*. Austin: University of Texas Press.

Walters, S.D.

1970. *Water for Larsa: An Old Babylonian Archive Dealing with Irrigation*. New Haven: Yale University Press.

Watson, J.L., ed.

1980. *Asian and African Systems of Slavery*. Oxford: Blackwell.

Watson, P.J., S.A. LeBlanc, and C.L. Redman.

1971. *Explanation in Archeology: An Explicitly Scientific Approach*. New York: Columbia University Press.

Watson, Philip.

1987. *Costume of Ancient Egypt*. New York: Chelsea House.

Watterson, Barbara.

1991. *Women in Ancient Egypt*. New York: St. Martin's.

Weber, Max.

1976. *The Agrarian Sociology of Ancient Civilizations*. London: NLB.

Wenig, Steffen.

1969. *The Women in Egyptian Art*. New York: McGraw-Hill.

Wenke, R.J.

1989. "Egypt: Origins of Complex Societies." *Annual Review of Anthropology* 18: 129–55.

Wheatley, Paul.

1971. *The Pivot of the Four Quarters: A Preliminary Enquiry into*

the Origins and Character of the Ancient Chinese City.
Edinburgh: Edinburgh University Press.

White, L.A.

1949. *The Science of Culture: A Study of Man and Civilization.*
New York: Grove.

1959. *The Evolution of Culture: The Development of Civilization
to the Fall of Rome.* New York: McGraw-Hill.

Wilk, R.R., and Wendy Ashmore, eds.

1988. *Household and Community in the Mesoamerican Past.*
Albuquerque: University of New Mexico Press.

Wilkinson, J.G.

1854. *A Popular Account of the Ancient Egyptians.* London: Murray.

Wilks, Ivor.

1975. *Asante in the Nineteenth Century: The Structure and Evolution of a Political Order.* Cambridge: Cambridge University
Press.

Willey, G.R.

1985. "Ancient Chinese-New World and Near Eastern Ideological
Traditions: Some Observations." *Symbols* (Spring Issue): 14–17,
22–23.

Wilson, J.A.

1960. "Egypt through the New Kingdom: Civilization without
Cities." In *City Invincible: A Symposium on Urbanization and
Cultural Development in the Ancient Near East.* C.H. Kraeling
and R.McC. Adams, eds. 124–64. Chicago: University of Chicago Press.

Wittfogel, K.A.

1957. *Oriental Despotism: A Comparative Study in Total Power.*
New Haven: Yale University Press.

Wolf, E.R., ed.

1976. *The Valley of Mexico: Studies in Pre-Hispanic Ecology and
Society.* Albuquerque: University of New Mexico Press.

Wylie, Alison.

1985. "The Reaction Against Analogy." In *Advances in Archaeological Method and Theory.* M.B. Schiffer, ed. 63–111. Orlando:
Academic Press.

Yoffee, Norman.
   1977. *The Economic Role of the Crown in the Old Babylonian Period.* Bibliotheca Mesopotamica, 5. Malibu: Undena.
Zantwijk, Rudolph van.
   1985. *The Aztec Arrangement: The Social History of Pre-Spanish Mexico.* Norman: University of Oklahoma Press.
Zuidema, R.T.
   1964. *The Ceque System of Cuzco: The Social Organization of the Capital of the Inca.* Leiden: Brill.
   1990. *Inca Civilization in Cuzco.* Austin: University of Texas Press.

Index

147